OPERATION DETACHMENT

1945 BATTLE OF IWO JIMA

DANIEL WRINN

CONTENTS

GET YOUR FREE COPY OF WW2: SPIES, SNIPERS AND THE WORLD AT WAR

Never miss a new release by signing up for my free readers group. Learn of special offers and interesting details I find in my research. You'll also get WW2: Spies, Snipers and Tales of the World at War delivered to your inbox. (You can unsubscribe at any time.) Go to danielwrinn.com to sign up.

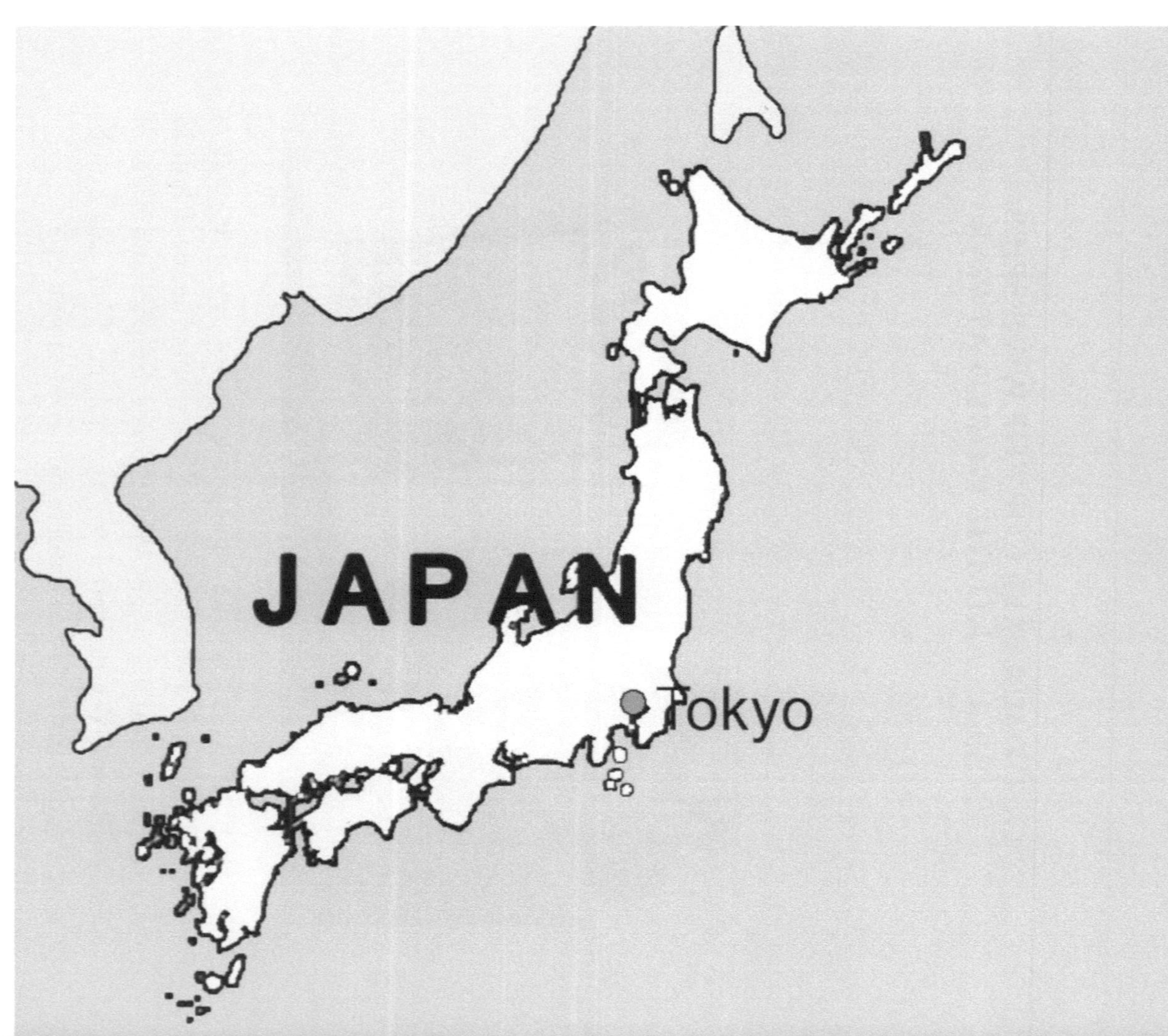
JAPAN
Tokyo

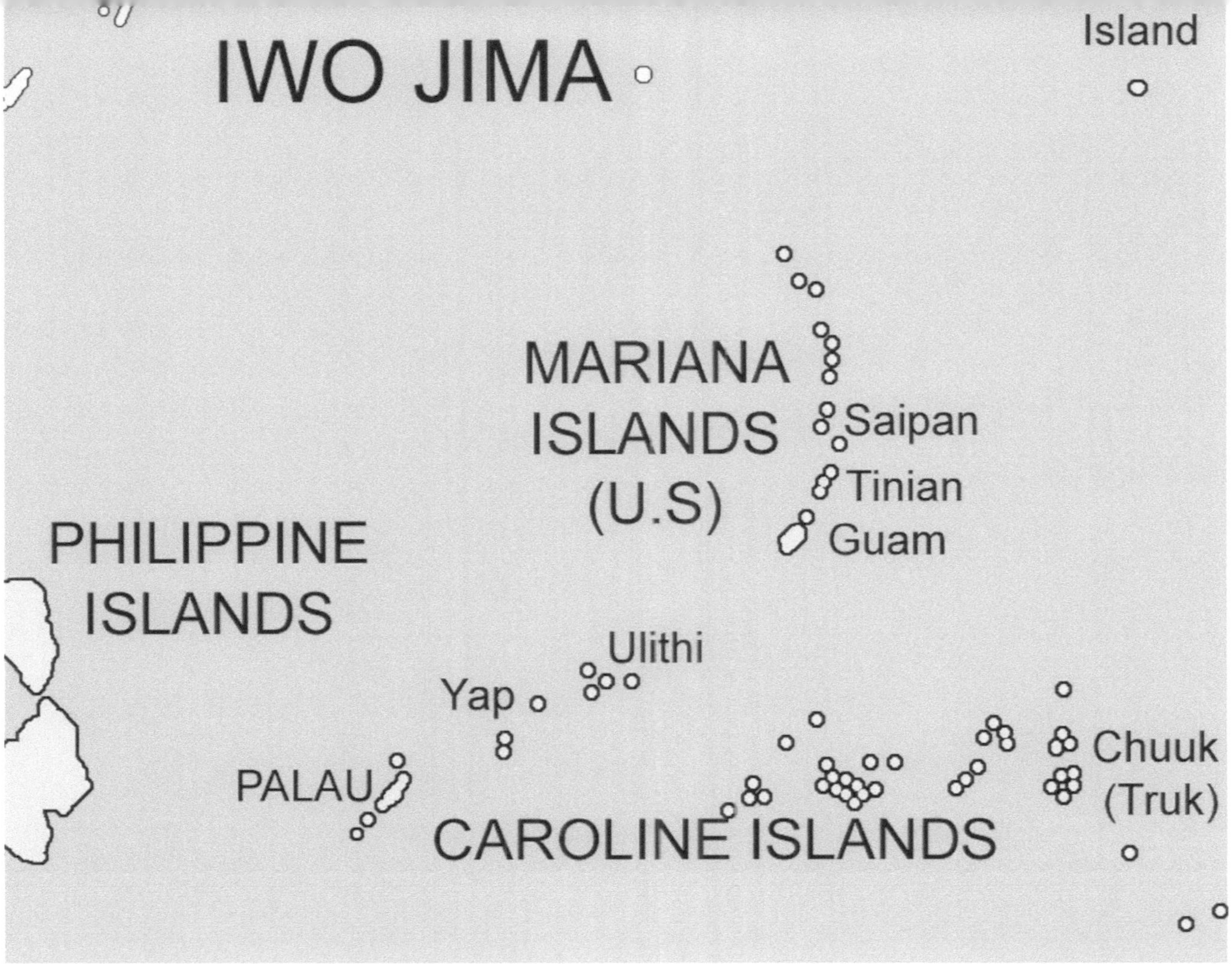

IWO JIMA

Island

MARIANA ISLANDS (U.S)

Saipan

Tinian

Guam

PHILIPPINE ISLANDS

Ulithi

Yap

PALAU

CAROLINE ISLANDS

Chuuk (Truk)

THE PACIFIC OFFENSIVE

March 4, 1945 was the second week of the Allied invasion of Iwo Jima. By now, the assault elements of the 3rd, 4th, and 5th Marine Divisions were drained, and their combat efficiency was seriously reduced.

The thrilling sight of the American flag being raised by the 28th Marines on Mount Suribachi had happened ten days earlier—a lifetime ago on Sulfur Island. The Amphibious Corps landing forces had already suffered 13,000 casualties, including 3,000 dead. The front was a jagged serration across Iwo Jima's fat northern half. Smack in the middle of the primary Japanese defenses. The Allied landing force had to advance uphill against a well-disciplined, entrenched, and rarely visible enemy.

In the center of the island, the 3rd Marine Division spent the night turning back a small, but determined, enemy counterattack, which found a gap between the 21st and 9th Marines. Savage hand-to-hand combat had cost both sides heavy casualties. The counterattack ruined the division's preparation for a morning advance, but both regiments made gains against stubborn enemy opposition.

In the east, the 4th Marine Division secured Hill 382 at the cost of their combat efficiency plummeting below fifty percent. By nightfall, it would fall another five percent. The 24th Marines, supported by flame-throwing tanks, only advanced one hundred yards before stopping to detonate two tons of explosives against enemy cave positions. The 23rd and 25th Marines entered the most challenging terrain yet—a broken ground with visibility less than a few feet.

On the western flank, the 5th Marine Division took Hill 362-B (Nishi Ridge) at the cost of over 500 casualties. They'd engaged a sizeable enemy force throughout the night. While the enemy attacks lacked coordination, exhausted Marines were barely able to hold them off. Most rifle companies were now at less than half strength. The division reported the net gain for the day as "practically nothing."

The battle took its toll on the enemy garrison as well. Japanese General Tadamichi Kuribayashi knew his *109th Division* had inflicted heavy casualties on the assaulting Marines, but his losses were comparable. The Allied capture of the critical hills the day before denied him his prized artillery observation sites.

Kuribayashi's brilliant chief of artillery, Colonel Chosaku Kaido, had been killed. Kuribayashi moved his command post from the central highlands to a large cave on the northwestern coast. Imperial Headquarters in Tokyo had reached him by radio that afternoon, but the general was in no mood for heroic rhetoric. He replied: "Send air and naval support, and I will hold the island. Without them, I cannot hold."

That afternoon, the combatants witnessed a glimpse of Iwo Jima's fate. Through the overcast skies, a giant silver bomber (the largest aircraft yet seen), the B-29 "Dinah Might," came in for an emergency landing on the scruffy island airstrip. Allied troops held their breath as the bomber swooped in and landed with a thud. Clipping a field telephone pole with its wing and rumbling to a stop three feet from the end of the strip.

Pilot Fred Malo and his ten-man crew didn't stay long. Every enemy gunner within range wanted to bag this prize. Mechanics made hurried field repairs, and the sixty-five-ton Super Fortress scrambled through a hail of enemy fire, returning to its base on Tinian.

The battle of Iwo Jima raged for another twenty-two days and claimed 11,000 more Allied casualties and the lives of nearly the entire Japanese garrison. A historic and colossal fight between two well-armed veteran forces. This was the bloodiest and biggest battle in the history of the Marine Corps. But after March 4, leaders on both sides had no doubts as to the ultimate outcome.

OPERATION DETACHMENT

Iwo Jima was an amphibious landing where assault troops saw the value of the objective. They were finally within a thousand miles of the Japanese homeland—and contributing clearly in support of the Allied bombing campaign.

This bombing campaign was a new wrinkle on an old theme. For forty years, Marines had been developing the skills to seize advanced naval bases in support of the fleet. In the Pacific war—especially at Tinian, Saipan, and now Iwo Jima—they secured advanced airbases to further the bombing of the Japanese home islands.

Allied forces had waited for the arrival of the B-29s for years. These long-range bombers became operational too late for the European Theater—but they'd been hitting Japan since November 1944 with disappointing results. The problem wasn't the planes or the pilots, but a little spit of volcanic rock halfway across the path from Saipan to Tokyo—Iwo Jima.

Radar on Iwo gave the enemy two hours' advance notice of every B-29 strike. Japanese fighters on Iwo's airfields would swarm and harass the unescorted Super Fortresses going in and especially returning to base. Enemy fighters picked off the B-29s crippled from antiaircraft fire. This caused the B-29s to fly higher and with a reduced payload.

The Joint Chiefs decided Iwo Jima must be secured with an Allied airfield built there. This would stop Japanese bombing raids and early warning interceptions. The airfield would offer fighter escorts through the treacherous portions of the B-29's missions and greater payloads at longer ranges. Iwo Jima in Allied hands would also provide emergency airfield support and landing for crippled B-29s returning from Tokyo and protect the Allied flank for the Okinawa invasion. Admiral Chester Nimitz was given three months to seize and develop Iwo Jima: codename Operation Detachment

Iwo Jima translates to "Sulfur Island" in Japanese. An ugly, foul-smelling, barren chunk of volcanic rock and sand—not even ten square miles in size. According to a Japanese Army officer: "an island of sulfur, no sparrow, no swallow, no water."

Less poetic Marines described Iwo's resemblance to a pork chop with a 556-foot volcano. Mount Suribachi dominated the southern end of the island and overlooked all potential landing beaches. Iwo rose unevenly over onto the Motoyama Plateau in the north before falling sharply off into the coast and steep cliffs and canyons. The northern terrain was a defender's dream: an intricate, broken, cave-dotted jungle of stone. Ringed by volcanic steam and a twisted landscape that seemed like a barren moon wilderness. More than one surviving Marine compared the eerie silence to something out of Dante's *Inferno*.

Iwo Jima in 1945 had two redeeming characteristics: the military value of its airfields and the psychological status of the island as a historical Japanese possession. The Allies were now within Japan's Inner Defense Zone. According to a Japanese officer: "Iwo Jima is the doorkeeper to the Imperial capital."

Even with the slowest aircraft, Tokyo could be reached in three flight hours from the island. In the Iwo Jima battle, 20,000 Allied and Japanese troops would be killed during brutal fighting in the last winter months of 1945.

No one suggested taking Iwo Jima would be easy. Admiral Nimitz assigned this mission to the same team who'd done so well in the earliest amphibious assaults in the Gilberts, Marshalls, and Marianas. Admiral Raymond Spruance would commend the 5th Fleet, Admiral Richmond Kelly Turner would commend the expeditionary forces, and Admiral Harry Hill would command the attack force.

Operation Detachment required unrelenting military pressure on the enemy and an accelerated planning schedule. The Amphibious task force preparing to assault Iwo Jima was getting squeezed on both ends. Admiral Hill desperately needed amphibious ships, shore bombardment vessels, and landing craft that were currently in use by General Douglas MacArthur and his reconquest of the Philippines. Poor weather and stiff enemy resistance combined to delay the completion of that operation.

The Joint Chiefs reluctantly postponed D-Day on Iwo from January 20 to February 19. The new schedule provided no relief for Allied planners. D-Day on Okinawa could be no later than April 1 because of the monsoon season. This tight timeframe held grim implications for Marine landing forces.

General Harry Schmidt would command the V Amphibious Corps in the assault. Schmidt's landing force consisted of three Marine divisions (3rd, 4th, and 5th). Schmidt would have the honor of commanding the largest US Marine force ever committed into a single battle—a force totaling over 80,000 troops.

Over half of these troops were Marine veterans from earlier fighting in the Pacific. Realistic training had prepared new Marines for the hard fight to come. The Iwo Jima assault force was arguably the most proficient amphibious force the world had yet to see.

Two senior Marines shared the limelight on Iwo Jima, and history has done them both an injustice. General Holland M. Smith, who then commanded the FMF (Fleet Marine Force), was tasked to participate in Operation Detachment as the Expeditionary Troops' Commanding General. This was an unnecessary billet. Schmidt had the rank, experience, staff, and resources to execute core level responsibility without being second-guessed.

General Smith was an amphibious pioneer and veteran of landings in the Gilberts, Marshalls, and the Marianas. According to him: "My sun had nearly set by then. I think they asked me along in case something happened to Harry Schmidt." Smith would try to keep out of Schmidt's way, but his decision to withhold the 3rd Marines (Expeditionary Troops Reserve) remains as controversial as it was in 1945.

General Smith proved himself an asset to the Iwo Jima campaign. He was always a voice in the wilderness in the top-level planning stage. Smith predicted severe casualties unless more effective preliminary naval bombardment was provided. He diverted visiting dignitaries and the press away from Schmidt and always offered a realistic counterpoint to some of the rosier staff estimates. According to Smith: "It's a tough proposition, that's why we're here."

General Schmidt's few public statements left him saddled with predicting Iwo Jima would be conquered in ten days. According to post-war accounts, Schmidt resented Smith's perceived role: "I was the commander of all troops on Iwo

Jima at all times. Holland Smith never had an onshore command post, never issued a single order, and never spent a single night ashore. Isn't it important from a historical standpoint that I commanded the greatest number of Marines ever to be engaged in a single action in the entire history of the Marine Corps?"

General Smith did not disagree with those points. While Smith proved to be useful, Schmidt and his staff should be credited for planning and executing the difficult and bloody Iwo Jima campaign.

The V Amphibious Corps' conquest of Iwo Jima was even more remarkable due to tough enemy opposition on the island. General Kuribayashi was one of the most fearsome opponents of the war. Kuribayashi was a fifth-generation samurai handpicked by the emperor. The Japanese general combined combat experience with an innovative mind and an iron will.

Although this would be his only struggle against US forces, he learned much about his opponents from earlier service in the US. Kuribayashi appraised with an unblinking eye the results of previous Japanese attempts to repel Allied invasions of Japanese-held garrisons.

Aside from the heroic rhetoric, Kuribayashi saw little value in the defend-at-the-water's-edge tactics and suicidal *banzai* attacks that branded Japan's failures from Tarawa to Tinian. Kuribayashi was a realist. He did not expect much help from Japan's depleted fleet and air forces. His best chance was to fortify Iwo's forbidding terrain with an in-depth defense, similar to the defense on Peleliu. Kuribayashi would shun coastal defenses, anti-landing, and banzai tactics. Instead, he'd wage a battle of attrition: a war of patience, nerves, and time. A delay and bleed strategy. Would the Allied forces lose heart and abandon the campaign?

A passive policy this late in the war was radical to senior Japanese Navy and Army leaders. It was counter to the deeply ingrained *Bushido* samurai code: a warrior code that viewed the defensive as only an unpleasant delay before the glorious offensive could resume—where the enemy would be destroyed by fire and sword. Imperial Headquarters was nervous. There was evidence of a top-level request for guidance in defending against Allied storm landings from Nazi Germany, whose experience trying to defend Normandy at the water's edge had proven disastrous.

Japanese command was unconvinced. Kuribayashi used his connection to the Emperor to avoid being relieved. But it was not a complete victory—the Navy insisted on building blockhouses and gun casements along the obvious landing beaches. Kuribayashi demanded assistance from the finest mining engineers and fortification specialists in the Empire.

The island favored the defender. Iwo's volcanic sand mixed with cement produced an exceptional concrete for installations. The soft rock was easy to dig. Over half of the Japanese garrison put their weapons aside and picked up picks and spades. When Allied bombers from the Seventh Air Force began a daily pummeling of the island in early December 1944, Kuribayashi just moved everything underground: weapons, command post, barracks, and aid stations. The engineering achievements he accomplished were extraordinary. Kuribayashi masked gun positions, created interlocking fields of fire, and miles of tunnels linking key defensive positions. Every cave had multiple outlets and ventilation tubes. One installation inside Mount Suribachi ran seven stories deep. Allied troops rarely encountered a live Japanese on the island until the bitter end.

Allied intelligence, aided by documents captured in Saipan and by an almost daily flow of aerial surveillance, was puzzled by the Japanese garrison's disappearing act. The photo interpreters, using stereoscopic lenses, listed 775 potential targets, but all were covered, hardened, and masked. Allied planners knew there was no fresh water available on the island. They saw the rainwater cisterns and knew what the average monthly rainfall would deliver. They determined the enemy garrison couldn't survive under those conditions in numbers greater than 12,000 for long. But Kuribayashi's force was twice that size. His troops had existed on half rations of water for months before the battle even began.

Unlike the earlier amphibious assaults on Guadalcanal and Tarawa, Allies would not have a strategic surprise on Iwo. Japanese headquarters believed Iwo would be invaded after the loss of the Marianas. Six months before the battle, Kuribayashi wrote to his wife: "the Americans will most definitely invade Iwo Jima—do not look for my return."

Kuribayashi ruthlessly worked his men to complete the defensive and training preparations by February 11, 1945. The general met his objective. Kuribayashi had a mixed force of recruits and veterans, soldiers and sailors. His artillerymen and mortar crews were the best in the Empire. Still, he trained and disciplined them all. Each fighting position had the commander's "Courageous Battle Vows" prominently posted above the firing apertures. Troops were cautioned to maintain their position and to take ten Marine lives for each Japanese death.

General Schmidt issued the operational plan on December 23, 1944. This plan wasn't fancy. Mount Suribachi towered over the potential landing beaches, but the 3,000 yards of black sand along the southeastern coast were more sheltered from the prevailing winds. It was here the V Amphibious Corps would land on D-Day. The 4th Marine Division on the right, the 5th on the left and the 3rd in reserve. The primary objectives were the lower airfield and Suribachi. Then, the assault force would swing into line and attack north shoulder to shoulder.

Anticipating a significant enemy counterattack on the first night, General Holland Smith said: “We welcome their counterattack. That’s generally when we break their back.”

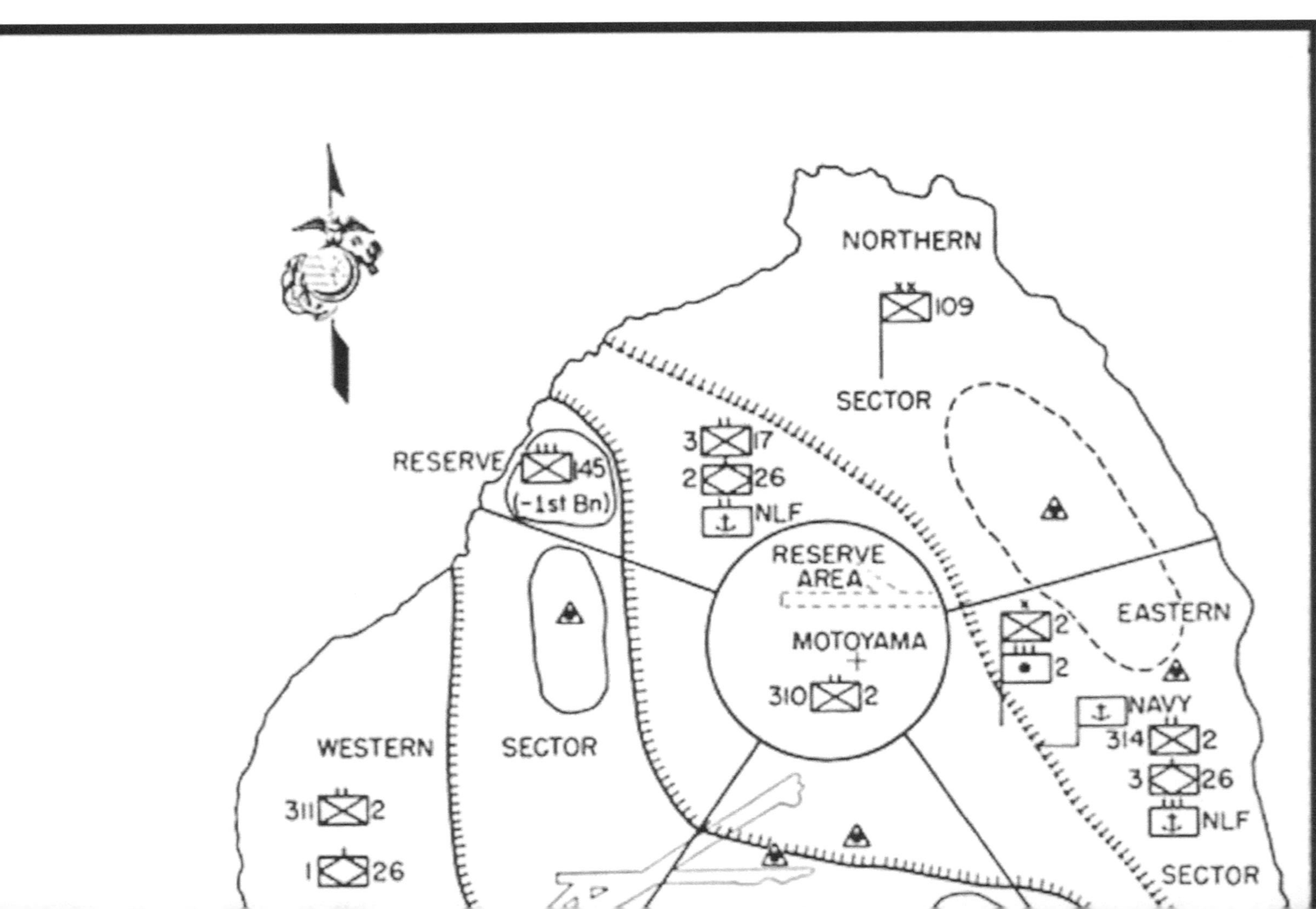
NORTHERN
109
SECTOR
RESERVE
145
(-1st Bn)
3 17
2 26
NLF
RESERVE AREA
MOTOYAMA
310 2
EASTERN
2
2
NAVY
314 2
3 26
NLF
SECTOR
WESTERN
SECTOR
311 2
1 26

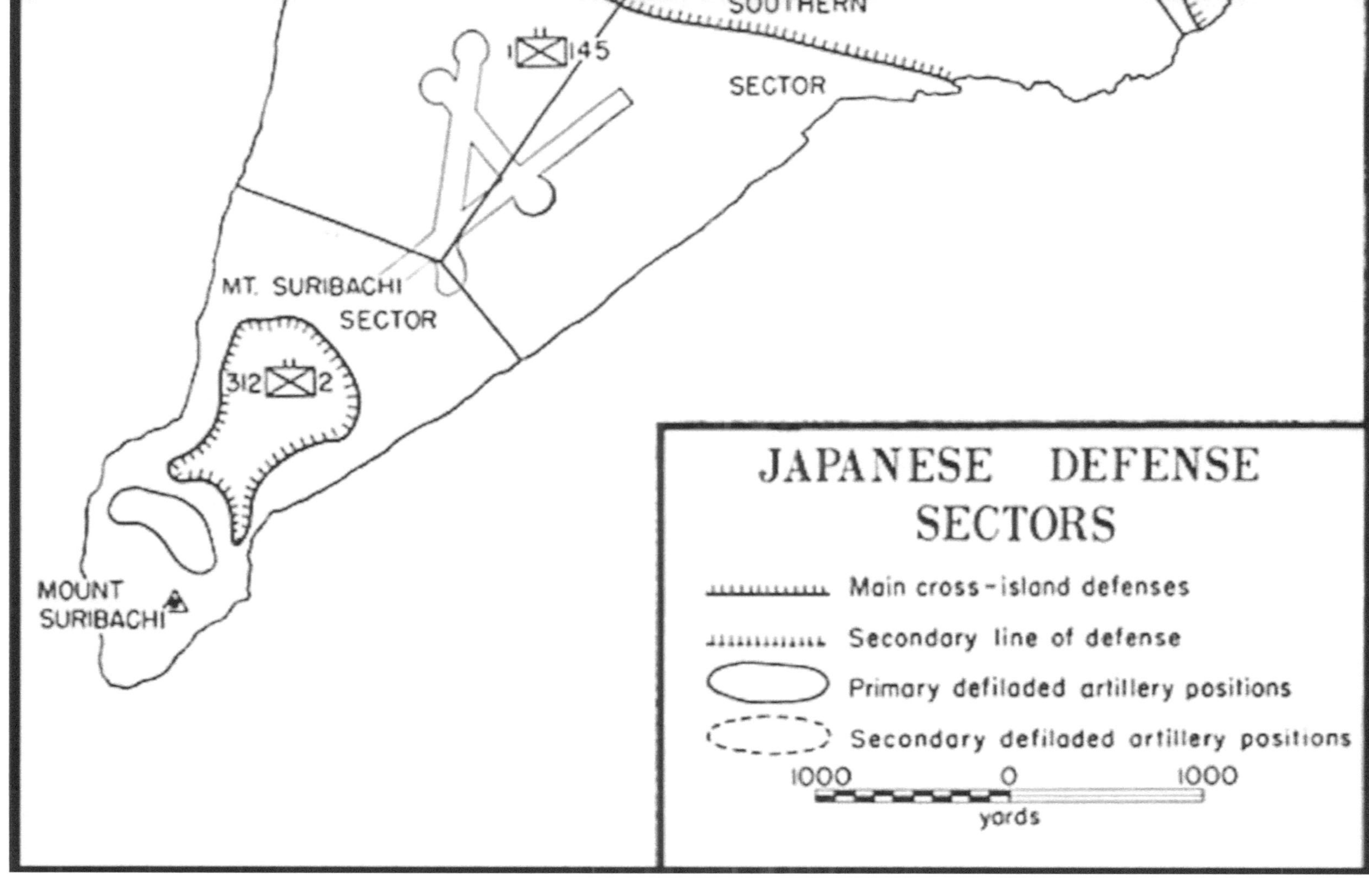
SOUTHERN
SECTOR
1
145
MT. SURIBACHI
SECTOR
312
2
MOUNT
SURIBACHI
JAPANESE DEFENSE
SECTORS
Main cross-island defenses
Secondary line of defense
Primary defiladed artillery positions
Secondary defiladed artillery positions
1000
0
1000
yards

KURIBAYASHI'S BIG MISTAKE

The physical separation of the three Marine divisions from Hawaii to Guam had no apparent adverse effect on their training. The proficiency of small units in combined arms assaults on fortified positions and amphibious landing were where it counted most. Each division was well prepared for the invasion.

The 3rd Marine Division had just completed their part in the liberation of Guam. Their field training often included active combat patrols to root out and destroy stubborn enemy survivors.

On Maui, the 4th Marine Division prepared for their fourth assault landing in thirteen months with quiet confidence. According to Major Fred Karch: "We had a continuity of veterans that was unbeatable."

The 5th Marine Division prepared for their first combat experience on the big island of Hawaii. The unit's newness would prove misleading. Over half of the officers and men were veterans, including several former Marine Raiders and Parachutists who'd fought in the Solomons. Colonel Don

Robertson took command of the 3rd Battalion, 27th Marine Regiment with less than two weeks before embarkation and immediately ordered them into the field for sustained live-fire exercises. Their confidence and competence impressed and convinced Robertson that these Marines were professionals.

Among the veterans preparing to deploy on Iwo Jima were two Medal of Honor recipients from Guadalcanal. Gunnery Sargent John Basilone and Colonel Robert Galer. The Marine Corps preferred to keep these distinguished veterans in the US for morale (bond raising) purposes, but both men wrangled their way back into the fight. Basilone led a machine gun platoon and Galer led a new radar unit for the Landing Force Air Support. The Guadalcanal veterans were amazed at the abundance of amphibious shipping available for Operation Detachment. Admiral Turner commanded 497 ships (140 of these were configured for amphib operations). This armada was ten times the size of the Guadalcanal task force.

But there were still problems. Many of the ships and crews were so new that each rehearsal featured an embarrassing collision or other accident. New bulldozers (TD-18s) were an inch too wide for the LCMs. Newly modified M4A3 Sherman tanks were so heavy that the LCMs rode with a dangerously low freeboard. The 105mm howitzers overloaded the DUKWs (amphibious trucks) to the point of unseaworthiness. These factors would soon prove treacherous in Iwo Jima's unpredictable surf.

Still, the massive Allied armada embarked and began the familiar move westward in good shape, well-trained, well-equipped, and thoroughly supported.

* * *

General Kuribayashi had benefited from the Allied delays of Operation Detachment due to the Philippines campaign. He felt as ready and prepared as possible. When the Allied armada sailed from the Marianas on February 13, he was warned. He deployed one infantry battalion into the lower airfield and ordered the bulk of his garrison into their assigned fighting holes—to await the inevitable storm.

Two issues divided the Navy/Marine team as D-Day on Iwo approached. The first was Admiral Spruance's decision to detach Task Force 58 (the fast attack carriers under Admiral Marc Mitscher) to attack strategic targets on Honshu (Main island of Japan) with the simultaneous bombardment of Iwo. Marine officers suspected a Navy/Air Force rivalry at work: Mitscher's targets were aircraft factories that the B-29s had missed a few days earlier. Mitscher took all eight Marine Corps fighter squadrons assigned to the fast carriers, plus the new fast battleships with their 16-inch guns. While Task Force 58 returned in time to offer fire support on D-Day, they were off again for good, two days later.

There was a continuing argument between senior Navy and Marine officers over the extent of the preliminary naval gunfire. Marines looked at their intelligence reports on Iwo Jima and requested ten days of preparatory fire. The Navy said it did not have the time nor the ammunition to spare; three days would have to suffice. Generals Smith and Schmidt pleaded their case to Admiral Spruance. Their request was denied. Admiral Spruance ruled that three days of preparatory fire along with the daily hammering administered by the Seventh Air Force would be good enough to get the job done.

Lieutenant Colonel Don Weller was the Task Force 51 naval gunfire officer, and no man knew the business more thoroughly than him. Weller had absorbed the Pacific War's lessons well. Especially the terrible failures at Tarawa. He argued the issue was not the weight of shells and other caliber but rather the time. The destruction of heavily fortified enemy targets took deliberate and pinpoint firing from close range. They had to be assessed and adjusted by aerial observers. His seven hundred plus hard targets would need time to knock out —a lot of time.

Admiral Spruance did not have time to give for strategic, tactical, and logistical reasons. Three days of firing would deliver four times the shells than Tarawa and would be one and a half time as much delivered against the larger Saipan. It would have to do.

Iwo's notoriously foul weather and strong enemy fortifications dissipated the three-day bombardment. According to General William Rogers: "We got about 13 hours with the fire support during the 34 hours of available daylight."

General Kuribayashi committed his only known tactical error during this battle. On D minus 2, a force of one-hundred Navy and Marine frogmen approached the eastern beaches. They were escorted by a dozen rocket-firing LCI (Landing Craft Infantry). Kuribayashi believed this was the main assault and authorized the coastal batteries to open fire. This exchange was hot and heavy with the LCIs getting the worst of it, but the US battleships and cruisers hurried to blast the casement guns that were suddenly revealed on Suribachi's right flank.

That night, seriously concerned about the hundreds of Japanese targets untouched by two days of firing, Admiral Turner authorized a "war council" on his flagship and junked the original plan. He ordered the gunships to concentrate exclusively on beach areas. This was done with considerable effect on D minus 1 and D-Day morning.

Kuribayashi noted most of the positions the Imperial Navy insisted on building along the beach were destroyed—just as he predicted. But his central defensive force that crisscrossed the Motoyama Plateau remained intact. "I pray for a heroic fight," Kuribayashi told his staff.

The press briefing held the night before D-Day on Admiral Turner's flagship was uncommonly somber. General Holland Smith predicted heavy casualties: upwards of 15,000, which shocked everyone. A man clad in khakis without a rank insignia then stood and addressed the room. It was the Secretary of the Navy, James Forrestal: "Iwo Jima, like Tarawa, leaves very little choice. Except to take it by force of arms, by character, and by courage."

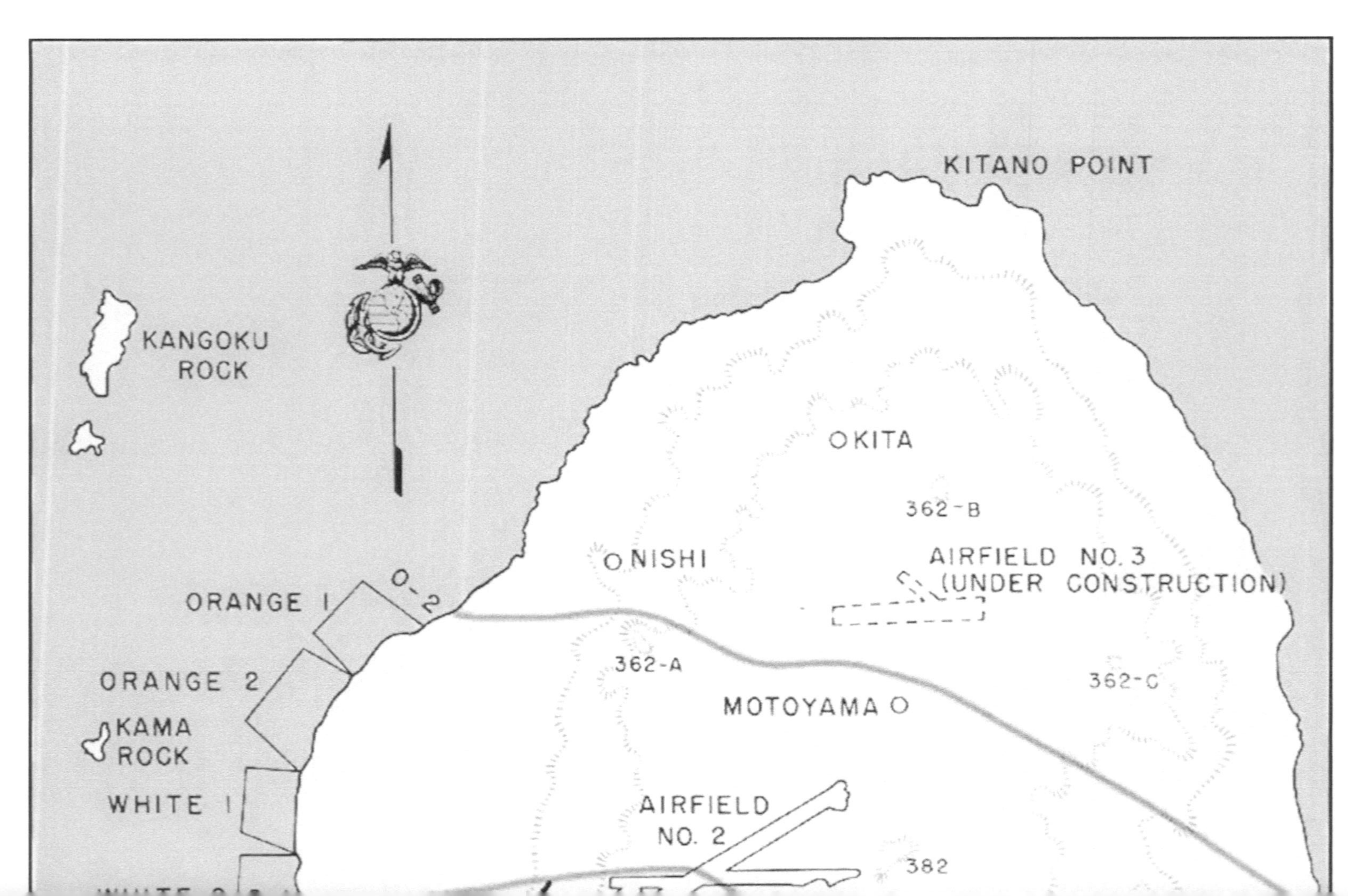

KITANO POINT
KANGOKU ROCK
OKITA
362-B
ONISHI
AIRFIELD NO. 3 (UNDER CONSTRUCTION)
O-2
ORANGE 1
ORANGE 2
362-A
362-C
MOTOYAMA
KAMA ROCK
WHITE 1
AIRFIELD NO. 2
382

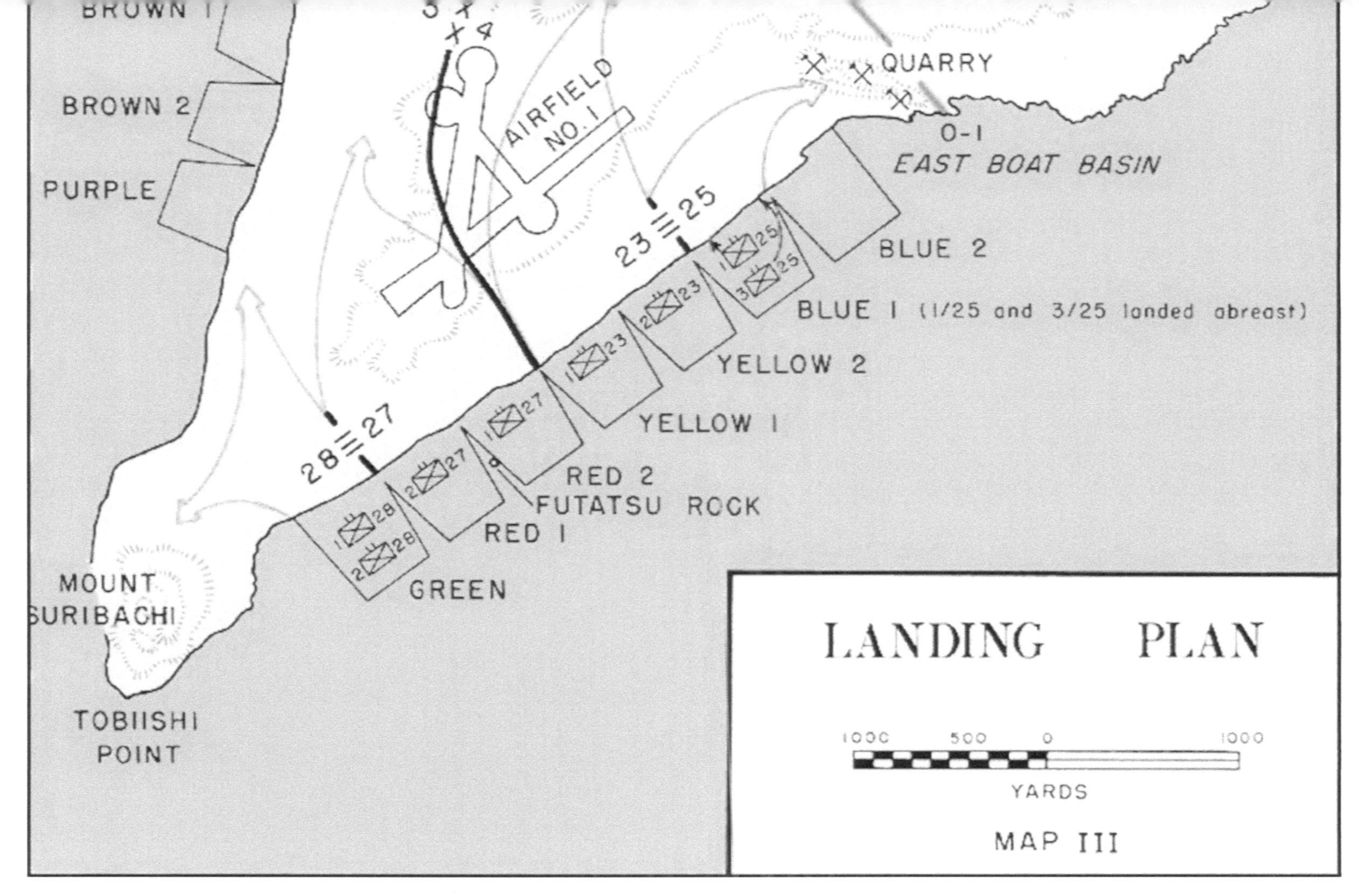
QUARRY
AIRFIELD NO. 1
BROWN 2
PURPLE
O-1
EAST BOAT BASIN
23 25
BLUE 2
BLUE 1 (1/25 and 3/25 landed abreast)
YELLOW 2
YELLOW 1
28 27
RED 2
FUTATSU ROCK
RED 1
GREEN
MOUNT SURIBACHI
TOBIISHI POINT
LANDING PLAN
1000 500 0 1000
YARDS
MAP III

D-DAY ON IWO JIMA

On D-Day morning, February 19, Iwo's weather conditions were ideal. At 0645, Admiral Turner signaled: "Land the landing force."

Shore bombardments had engaged the enemy island at near point-blank range. Battleships and cruisers steamed in as close as 1,500 yards to level their guns against their island targets. Many of these older battleships had performed this dangerous mission in other theaters of the war. The *Nevada,* raised from the muck and ruin of Pearl Harbor, led the bombardment force. The battleship *Arkansas,* built in 1912, had joined the armada from the Atlantic where she'd battered German positions at Normandy during the Allied landing on June 6, 1944.

Colonel "Bucky" Buchanan devised a modified form of the "rolling barrage" used by the bombarding gunships against beachfront targets. This concentration of naval gunfire advanced gradually as troops landed. Always 400 yards to the front. Air spotters would regulate the pace. This innovation was appealing to the division commanders who'd served in

World War I France. In those days, a rolling barrage was often the only way to break a stalemate.

The amount of shelling was shocking. Admiral Hill later wrote: "there were no proper targets for shore bombardment remaining on D-Day morning." This was an overstatement. No one denied the fury of firepower delivered against the landing beaches and surrounding areas. General Kuribayashi admitted in an assessment report to Imperial headquarters: "we need to reconsider the power of bombardment from ships. The violence of enemy bombardments is far beyond description."

When the task force appeared over the horizon, troop ships crowded with combat-equipped Marines gazed at the stunning fireworks. The Guadalcanal veterans among them watched with grim satisfaction as battleships hammered the island. The world had come full circle from the dark days of October 1942: when the 1st Marines and the Cactus Air Force suffered a similar shelling from Japanese battleships.

Sailors and Marines were eager to get their first glimpse of the objective. War correspondent John Marquand wrote of his first impressions on Iwo: "a silhouette like a sea monster, with a little dead volcano for a head and the beach area for the neck and a scrubby brown cliff for the body."

Navy Lieutenant David Susskind wrote his thoughts from the bridge of the troopship *Mellette*: "Iwo Jima was an ugly and rude sight. Only a geologist could look at it and not be disgusted."

A surgeon in the 25th Marines, Lieutenant Mike Keleher wrote: "the naval bombardment had already begun. I saw the orange-yellow flashes as the cruisers, battleships, and destroyers blasted away at the island with broadsides. We were close to Iwo, just like the pictures and models we'd been studying for weeks. A volcano was on our left and long flat beaches in a rough, rocky plateau was on our right."

General Clifton Cates studied the island through binoculars from his ship. Each division would land two reinforced regiments abreast. From left to right, the beaches were designated Green, Red, Yellow, and Blue. The 5th Division would land the 27th and 28th Marines on the left flank on Green and Red Beaches, While the 4th would land the 23rd and 25th Marines on the right flank at Blue Beach.

General Schmidt reviewed the latest intelligence reports with growing anxiety and requested that General Holland Smith reassign the reserve forces. Schmidt wanted the 3/21 Marines to replace the 26th Marines as the core reserve and release them to the 5th Division. Schmidt envisioned the 28th Marines cutting the island in half before turning to capture Suribachi. The 25th would scale the rock quarry, serving as the hinge for the entire corps to swing north. The 23rd and 27th Marines would then capture the first airfield, before pivoting north into their assigned zones.

General Cates was concerned about Blue Beach on the right flank. Blue Beach was directly under the observation and fire of suspected enemy positions in the rock quarry. Steep cliffs overshadowed their right flank, while Suribachi dominated the left. The 4th Division figured that the 25th Marines would have the most challenging objective to take on D-Day. General Cates said: "if I knew the name of the man on the extreme right of that squad, I'd recommend him for a medal before we even get there."

Iwo Jima was the pinnacle of a forced amphibious landing against a heavily fortified shore. A complex art mastered by the Fifth Fleet through many painstaking campaigns. B-24 bombers from the Seventh Air Force flew in to strike the smoking island. Rocket ships moved in to saturate shore targets. Fighter and attack squadrons from Mitscher's Task Force 58 joined in. While Navy pilots showed their skills at bombing and strafing, the troops started cheering at the sight of F4U Corsairs flown in from Marine fighter squadron 213.

Colonel Vernon McGee was the air officer for the Expeditionary Troops. He urged this special show for the men in the assault waves. "Drag your bellies on the beach," McGee said to the Marine fighters. The F4U Corsairs made an aggressive approach parallel to the island. They streaked low over the beaches and savagely strafed enemy targets. The Pacific War geography since Bougainville kept ground Marines separated from their air support. According to McGee: "it was the first-time many troops had ever seen a Marine fighter plane, and they were not disappointed."

Not long after the planes left, naval gunfire resumed. Gunfire carpeted the beach with a crescendo of high explosive shells. Ship-to-shore movement was underway, an easy thirty-minute run for the LVTs.

For Operation Detachment, there were enough LVTs to get the job done. Sixty-eight LVT (A)4 armored amtracs, with snub-nosed 75mm cannons, blasted the way forward with 385 troop laden LVTs following close behind. The assault waves crossed the line of departure on time and confidently chugged toward the smoking beaches.

On Iwo, there was no coral reef or killer neap tides to worry about. Navy frogmen cleared the approaches of tetrahedrons and mines. There was no premature secession of fire. The modified rolling barrage was in effect, and no vehicles were lost from enemy fire. Assault waves hit the beaches within two minutes of H-hour. Enemy observers watching the drama unfold from a cave on the slopes of Suribachi reported: "At 9 am, several hundred landing craft with amphibious tanks rushed toward shore like an enormous tidal wave."

Colonel Robert Williams, XO of the 28th Marines, later wrote: "The landing was a magnificent sight to see—two divisions landing abreast—you could see the whole show from the deck of a ship. At this point, so far so good."

The first obstacle didn't come from the Japanese, but from the beach and its parallel terraces. Iwo was a volcano with steep beaches that sharply dropped off into a narrow and violent surf zone. Soft black sand immobilized all wheeled vehicles and caused many tracked amphibious vehicles to belly down and get stuck.

The following boat waves had even more trouble. When ramps dropped and a Jeep or truck would drive out, they got stuck too. Then, plunging waves would smash into the stalled craft before they could unload, filling their sterns with water and sand and broaching them broadside. The beach quickly became a salvage yard.

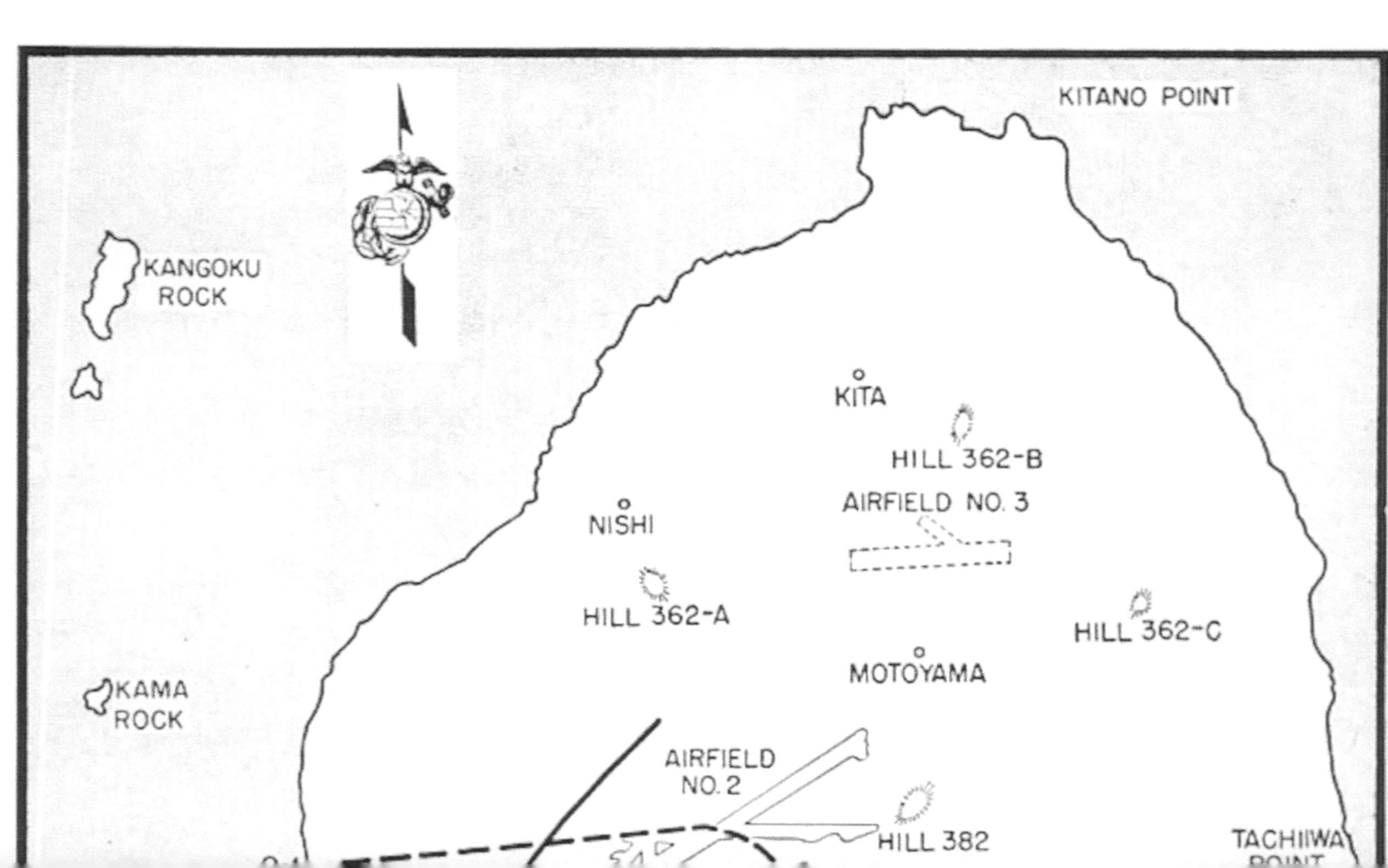
KITANO POINT
KANGOKU ROCK
KITA
HILL 362-B
AIRFIELD NO. 3
NISHI
HILL 362-A
HILL 362-C
MOTOYAMA
KAMA ROCK
AIRFIELD NO. 2
HILL 382
TACHIIWA

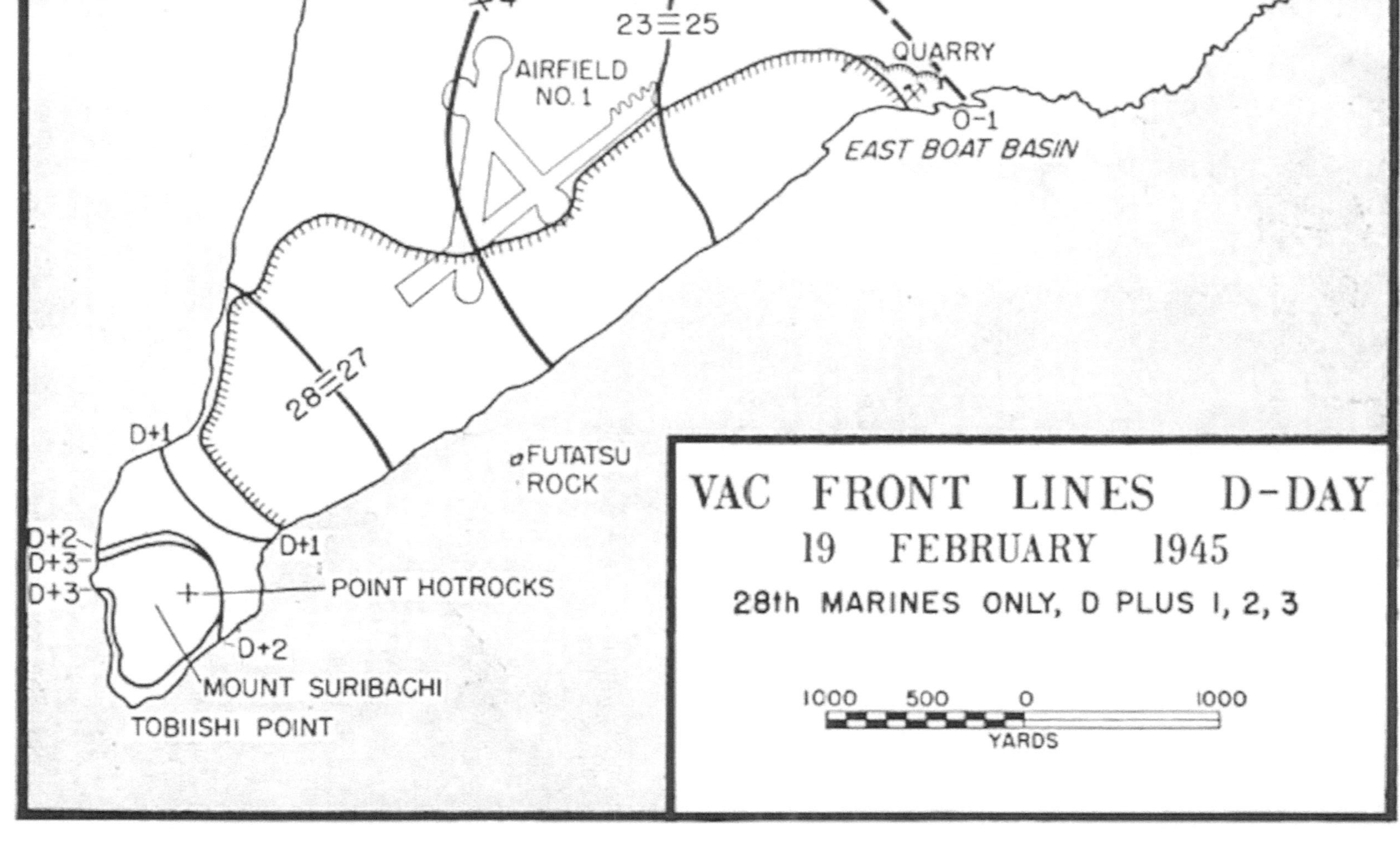

VAC FRONT LINES D-DAY
19 FEBRUARY 1945
28th MARINES ONLY, D PLUS 1, 2, 3
1000 500 0 1000
YARDS
23≡25
AIRFIELD NO. 1
QUARRY
O-1
EAST BOAT BASIN
28≡27
D+1
D+1
D+2
D+3
D+3
D+2
FUTATSU ROCK
POINT HOTROCKS
MOUNT SURIBACHI
TOBIISHI POINT

GETTING THE GUNS ASHORE

The heavily laden infantry was bogged down. According to Corporal Ed Hartman, a rifleman in the 4th Marine Division: "the sand was so soft, it was like trying to run in loose coffee grounds." The 28th Marines' first report after getting ashore: "resistance moderate, terrain awful."

The rolling barrage and carefully executed landing produced the desired effect: suppressing enemy fire while providing enough shock and awe to allow the first assault waves to clear the beach and advance inward. In less than fifteen minutes, 6,000 Marines were ashore. Many were hampered by increasing fire over the terraces and down from the highlands, but hundreds leaped forward and maintained their assault momentum.

The 28th Marines on the left flank had rehearsed this landing on the volcanic terrain of Hawaii's Big Island. Now, despite increasing casualties among company commanders and the usual landing disorganization, elements of the regiment used their initiative to advance across the narrow neck of the peninsula. This became much bloodier as enemy strong points along Suribachi's base sprung to life.

Ninety minutes after landing, elements of the 1/28 Marines reached the western shore—700 yards from Green Beach—Iwo had been severed. According to one Marine: "it was like we cut off the snake's head." This was the deepest penetration of what would become a costly and bloody day.

The regiments had difficulty getting across the black-sand terraces toward the airfield. The terrain was like an open bowl in a shooting gallery. In full view of Suribachi on the left and a rising table to the right. Any thoughts of this operation being a cakewalk quickly vanished as registered machine gun fire whistled across the open ground and mortar rounds dropped along the terraces. Through this hardship, the 27th Marines made good initial gains and reached the southern and western edges of the first airfield by noon.

The 23rd Marines on Yellow Beach took the brunt of the first round of enemy combined arms fire. Troops crossing the terrace were confronted by two massive concrete pillboxes—still lethal after the bombardment. Overcoming these positions proved costly in men and time and. More fortified positions rose from the broken ground beyond. Requests for tank support could not be fulfilled because of the congestion problems on the beach. Still, the regiment clawed its way several hundred yards toward the eastern edge of the airstrip.

The 25th Marines immediately ran into a "Buzz-Saw" trying to move across Blue Beach. General Cates was correct in his appraisal: "The right flank was a bitch, if there ever was one." The 1/25 Marines scratched, scrambled, and clawed their way 300 yards forward under heavy enemy fire in the first half-hour. The 3/25 Marines took the heaviest beating of the day on the extreme right flank while trying to scale the cliffs leading to the rock quarry.

According to Lieutenant Colonel Justice Chambers leading the 3/25 Marines: "Crossing that second terrace, there was fire from automatic weapons coming from all over. I could've held up a cigarette and lit it on the stuff going by. I knew immediately we were in for one hell of a fight."

But this was only the beginning. When the landing forces tried to overcome the enemy's infantry weapons, they were blind to an imperceptible stirring taking place among the rocks and crevices in the interior highlands. General Kuribayashi's gunners unmasked their big guns—giant mortars, heavy artillery, rockets, and antitank weapons held under the tightest discipline for just this precise moment. Kuribayashi had waited patiently until the beaches were clogged with troops and material. Gun crews knew the range and deflection at each landing beach by heart: all weapons had been pre-registered on these targets long ago. At Kuribayashi's signal, hundreds of weapons opened fire. It was shortly after 1030.

This bombardment was as horrifying and deadly as any Marines had ever experienced. There was no cover. Enemy mortar and artillery rounds blanketed every corner of the 3,000-yard-wide beach. Large caliber coastal defense guns and dual-purpose antiaircraft guns fired horizontally. This created a deadly scissor of direct fire from high ground on both flanks. Marines stumbled over the terraces to escape the rain of lethal projectiles only to encounter machine-gun fire and minefields. Landing force casualties mounted at a shocking rate.

Major Karch of the 14th Marines expressed a begrudging admiration for the Japanese gunners: "it was one of the worst blood-lettings of the war. They rolled artillery barrages up and down the beach—I don't see how anybody could've lived through such a heavy fire barrage. The Japanese were superb artillerymen—someone was going to get hit every time they fired."

At sea, naval gunfire support desperately tried to deliver fire against enemy gun positions shooting down from the rock quarry. It took longer to coordinate this fire: the first enemy barrages wiped out the entire 3/25 Marines Shore Fire Control Party.

When the Japanese fire reached a crescendo, assault regiments issued grim reports to the flagship. Within fifteen minutes, these messages buzzed over the command net:

From 25th Marines 1036: Catching hell from the quarry. Heavy mortar and machine-gun fire.

From the 23rd Marines 1039: Taking heavy casualties and cannot move forward. Mortars are killing us.

From the 27th Marines 1042: All units pinned down by mortars and artillery. Heavy casualties. Need tank support fast to move.

From the 28th Marines 1046: Taking heavy fire and forward movement stopped. Artillery and machine-gun fire heaviest yet seen.

The landing force was getting bled but did not panic. The abundance of combat veterans throughout the rank-and-file beach regiments helped the rookies focus on the objective. Communications were still effective. Aerial observers spotted some of the now exposed gun positions and directed effective naval gunfire. Carrier planes screeched in low and dropped napalm from their belly tanks. But heavy enemy fire continued to take an awful toll throughout the first day and night—but would never again be as murderous as that first hour.

Sherman tanks played hell getting into the action on D-Day. Later in the battle, these combat vehicles were the most valuable weapons on the battlefield. This day was a nightmare. The assault divisions had embarked many tanks on board LSMs (Landing Ship Medium), sturdy craft that could deliver five Shermans at a time. But it was a challenge to disembark them on Iwo's steep beaches. The LSMs' stern anchors couldn't hold in the loose sand and the bow cables parted under the strain.

One lead tank stalled on top of the ramp and blocked the others, leaving the LSM at the mercy of the violent surf. Other tanks threw tracks or got bogged down in loose sand. Several tanks that made it over the terraces were destroyed by huge horn mines or were disabled by accurate 47mm antitank fire from Suribachi. Still, the tanks kept coming. Their mobility, armor protection, and 75mm guns were a welcome addition to the scattered infantry along Iwo's lunar-looking, shell-pocked landscape.

The division commanders committed their reserves. The 26th Marines were ordered in just after noon, General Cates ordered two battalions of the 24th Marines to land at 1400. The 3/24 Marines followed several hours later. The reserve suffered heavier casualties than the initial assault units crossing the beach, because of the punishing enemy bombardment from all island points.

Aware of a probable Japanese counterattack in the night to come, and despite the fire and confusion along the beaches, both divisions ordered their artillery regiments ashore. This frustrating and costly process took most of the afternoon. The surf and wind picked up as the day wore on and caused more than one low-riding amphibious truck to swamp with its precious 105mm howitzer cargo. Getting the guns ashore was one thing; getting them up off the sand was another.

The 75mm howitzers did better than the heavier 105s. Marines could quickly move them up over the terraces—at significant risk. But the 105s had a mind of their own in the black sand. The effort to get each weapon off the beach was a saga. Despite unforgiving terrain and enemy fire, Marines managed to get the batteries in place and registered them to render close-fire support before dark.

Plunging surf and enemy fire turned the battlefield into utter chaos. Later that afternoon, Lieutenant Mike Keleher, the battalion surgeon, went ashore to take over the aid station. (A sniper had killed the previous surgeon.) Lieutenant Keleher was a veteran of three assault landings. He was shocked by the carnage on Blue Beach: "such a sight on the beach. Wrecked boats, bogged down jeeps and tractors and tanks. Burning vehicles and casualties. Limbs of dead Marines were scattered all over the beach."

PROWLING WOLVES

An enemy mortar shell took the life of the legendary John Basilone. He'd led his machine gun platoon in a brave attack against the southern portion of the airfield. All Marines on the island felt this loss. Farther east, Colonel Rob Galer (one of the Pacific War's first fighter aces) survived the afternoon's battle along the beaches and reassembled his scattered radar unit in a deep shell-hole near the base of Suribachi.

Later that afternoon, Colonel Donn Robertson led his Marines onshore to Blue Beach. He was shocked at the intensity of fire still directed at the troops so late on D-Day: "they were ready for us. I watched with pride and wonderment as young Marines landed under fire, took casualties, and stumbled forward to clear the beach. I asked myself, what impels a young man landing on the beach in the face of fire?"

Then it was Robertson's turn. His boat slammed into the beach too hard. The ramp wouldn't drop. His Marines had to roll over the gunwales into the churning surf and crawl ashore.

The savage battle to capture the rock quarry cliffs on the right flank raged. The beachhead was exposed to direct enemy fire all day. Marines had to storm them before any more supplies or troops could be landed. In the end, it was the fighting spirit of Captain James Headley and Colonel "Jumping Joe" Chambers who led the survivors of the Marines to the top of the cliffs.

The battalion paid a high price for this feat. They'd lost twenty-two officers and five hundred troops by nightfall. Assistant division commanders Generals Hart and Hermle of the 4th and 5th Marine Division spent most of D-Day on board the control vessels marking both ends of the line a departure—4,000 yards offshore. This was another lesson in amphibious techniques learned from Tarawa. Having senior officers close to the ship-to-shore movement provided landing force decision-making from the forward most vantage point.

By dust, General Hermle chose to come ashore. On Tarawa, he'd spent the night of D-Day out of contact on a fire-swept pierhead. This time he would be in the fight.

Hermle had the bigger operational picture in mind. He understood that the corps' commanders insistence on forcing the reserves and artillery units onshore despite the carnage to build combat power. Hermle knew that whatever the night brought, the Allies had more troops on the island than the Japanese could muster. His presence would help his division forget about the earlier days' disaster and focus on preparing for the inevitable enemy counterattacks.

Enemy mortar and artillery fire raked the beachhead. An enormous spigot of mortar shells (Marines called them "flying ashcans") and rocket-boosted aerial bombs were loud, whistling projectiles that tumbled end over end. Many of them sailed over the island, but those that landed along the beaches of the southern runways caused dozens of casualties. Few Marines could dig a proper foxhole in the sand. It was like trying to dig a hole in a barrel of wheat. With urgent calls to the control ship for plasma and stretchers and mortar shells came repeated sandbag requests.

War combat correspondent Lieutenant Cyril Zurlinden (soon to become a casualty himself) described his first night ashore: "On Tarawa, Saipan, and Tinian, I saw Marines killed and wounded in a shocking manner. But I never saw anything like the ghastliness that hung over the Iwo Jima beachhead. It was utter frustration, anguish, and a constant inner battle to maintain at least some semblance of sanity.

Accounting for personnel was a nightmare under those conditions. But assault divisions eventually reported a combined loss of 2,375 men to General Schmidt—503 killed and 1,755 wounded, 18 missing, and 99 combat fatigues. While these statistics were sobering, Schmidt had gotten

30,000 Marines ashore. A casualty rate of eight percent left the landing force in better condition than Saipan or Tarawa's first day. It was a miracle the casualties hadn't been twice as high. Did Kuribayashi wait too long to use his big guns?

The first night in Iwo Jima was an eerie affair. Mists of sulfur spiraled from the earth. Marines who were used to the tropics now shivered in the cold, waiting for Kuribayashi's samurai warriors to come screaming down the hills. Marines learned this Japanese commander was different. There would be no wasteful banzai attack tonight. Instead, small teams of infiltrators, "Prowling Wolves," would probe the Marine lines and gather intelligence. A barge full of the elite Japanese *Special Landing Forces* tried a counter landing on the western beaches—they died to a man under the alert guns of the 28th Marines and supporting LVT crews.

That night was one of continuous indirect fire from the Highlands. A high velocity round landed directly in a fighting hole occupied by the 1/23 Marines commander Colonel Ralph Hass and instantly killed him. Marines took other light casualties throughout the night, but at dawn, the veteran landing force stirred.

Five infantry regiments moved to the north, while the sixth turned to the business at hand in the south: Mount Suribachi

SURIBACHI-YAMA

Marines knew this dormant volcano as "Hotrocks."

The Japanese called it Suribachi-yama. Allied planners knew their drive north would never succeed without first securing that hulking rock dominating the southern plain. According to one Marine: "Suribachi took on a life of its own. It watched over us. It loomed over us. That mountain represented more evil to us than the Japanese."

Colonel Atsuchi commanded 2,000 enemy soldiers and sailors in the Suribachi garrison. The Japanese had honeycombed the mountain with machine-gun nests, tunnels, and observation sites. But Atsuchi had lost many of his large-caliber guns from the three-day naval bombardment. Atsuchi's command at Suribachi was semiautonomous. General Kuribayashi realized the invaders would soon cut communication lines across the island's narrow tip. Kuribayashi hoped Atsuchi could hold out for at least ten days and maybe even two weeks.

Some of the strongest defenses on Suribachi were down along the rubble-strewn base. Here, over seventy camouflaged concrete blockhouses protected the mountain's approaches. Another fifty blockhouses bulged from the slopes within the first hundred feet of elevation. Then came the caves, and the first of hundreds the Marines would face on Iwo Jima.

The 20th Marines took 407 casualties cutting across the neck of the island on D-Day. The following day in a cold rain, they prepared their assault. Colonel Chandler Johnson, commanding the 2/28 Marines, set the morning's tone as he deployed his tired troops forward: "it's going to be a hell of a day in one hell of a place to fight this damn war."

Several 105mm batteries opened up overhead. Gun crews fired from positions dug in the black sand next to the 28th Marine's command post. Troops learned that even their 155mm howitzers would hardly shiver the enemy's concrete pillboxes. As the preparatory fire lifted, infantry advanced into heavy mortar and machine-gun fire. Colonel "Harry the Horse" Liversedge requested tanks. But the 5th Tank Battalion was having a frustrating morning. Tanks desperately searched for a defilade spot to rearm and refuel for the assault. But in those first few days on Iwo, there was no such spot. Every time the tanks gathered to service their vehicles, they were walloped by enemy artillery and mortar fire from the entire island. Getting the tanks serviced to join in on the assault took most of the morning. After getting battered all day, the tankers would now only refit, rearm, and re-equip at night.

The day's slow start led to more setbacks for the 5th Tank Battalion. Enemy antitank gunners hid in the hodgepodge of boulders and knocked out the first approaching Shermans, crippling the assault's momentum. While the 20th Marines overran forty enemy strongpoints and gained 200 yards a day, they lost a Marine for every yard gained. The tankers redeemed themselves when a 75mm round caught Colonel Atsuchi poking his head out of a cave entrance—blowing him apart.

Elsewhere on the morning of D +1 were discouraging sites of chaos along the beaches from Kuribayashi's unrelenting artillery barrages and the violent surf. According to one Marine: "The wreckage was indescribable. I saw two miles of debris that was so thick there were only a few places our landing craft could still get in. The wrecked hulls of dozens of landing boats testified to the price we had to pay to put our troops ashore. Tanks and half-tracks laid there crippled from getting bogged down in the coarse sand. LVTs and amphibian tractors were victims of mines and well-aimed shells and were now flopped on their backs. Cranes were brought in to unload cargo and were tilted at insane angles. Our bulldozers were smashed in their own roadways."

Then bad weather set in and complicated the unloading.

Strong winds whipped sea swells into a nasty chop. The surf got uglier. These were the conditions Colonel Carl Youngdale faced while trying to land the 105mm howitzer batteries of his 4/14 Marines. All twelve of these guns were preloaded in amphibious trucks (DUKWs) one to a vehicle. Adding to that was the problem of marginal seaworthiness and contaminated fuel. Youngdale watched in shock as eight amphibious trucks suffered engine failures, swamped, and sank with a terrible loss of life. Two more amphibious trucks broached in the surf zone and spilled their guns into deep water. Youngdale managed to get the two remaining guns ashore and into firing position.

General Schmidt committed one battery of the 105mm howitzers to the narrow beachhead on D +1. These guns reached the beach intact, but it took hours to get the amphibious tractors to drag the heavy guns up over the terraces. The 105's were in place and firing before dark. The deep bark of the guns was a welcome sound to the Marines. Concerned about heavy casualties in the first twenty-four hours, General Schmidt committed the 21st Marines from the core reserve. But the seas were too rough. Troops had a harrowing experience trying to climb down the cargo nets and into the small boats—violently bobbing alongside the transports. Many Marines tumbled into the sea. The boating process took hours to complete. Once afloat, troops circled endlessly in the small Higgins boats waiting for the call to land. But after six hours of bobbing in the water and awful seasickness, the 21st Marines returned to the ships for the night.

Even the larger landing craft, the LSMs and LCTs, had a hard time breaching. Sea anchors were needed to keep the craft perpendicular to the breakers, and they rarely held fast in that soft bottom. Admiral Hill later wrote: "dropping that stern anchor was like dropping a spoon in a bowl of mush."

Hill contributed to the development of amphibious operations in the Pacific War. He and his staff developed armored bulldozers to land in the assault waves. They experimented with hinged *Marston* matting, used as a temporary road on airfields to get vehicles over soft sand. On the beach at Iwo, bulldozers were worth their weight in gold. The Marston matting was only partially successful: the LVTs chewed it up, but all hands could see the true potential.

Admiral Hill worked with the Naval Construction Battalion (Seabees) to bring the supply-laden pontoon barges ashore. But again, the surf prevailed and broached the craft, spilling the cargo. Now desperate, Hill's beachmasters turned to a round-the-clock use of amphibious trucks and LVTs to keep the combat cargo flowing. Once amphibious trucks got free of their crippling loads, they were fine.

Amphibian tractors could cross the soft beach without help. They resupplied and conducted medevac missions directly along the front lines. These vehicles suffered from inexperienced crews in the LSTs who wouldn't lower their bow ramps enough to accommodate the amphibious trucks and tractors approaching after dark. Many times, vehicles loaded with wounded Marines got lost in the dark or ran out of gas and sank. The amphibian tractor battalions lost over 147 LVTs at Iwo Jima. Unlike Tarawa, where enemy gunfire and mines accounted for less than twenty percent of this total. Thirty-four LVTs perished from Iwo's crushing surf, and eighty-eight sank in the deep water.

Once ashore and clear of the loose sand along the beaches, half-tracks, tanks, and armored bulldozers collided with the strongest minefield defenses yet encountered in the Pacific. Under Kuribayashi's direction, enemy engineers had planted irregular rows of antitank and horned anti-boat mines along the exits from both beaches.

The enemy accompanied these weapons by rigging

massive makeshift explosives from 500-pound aerial bombs, torpedo heads, and depth charges triggered by a pressure mine. The loose soil on Iwo had enough metallic characteristics to render standard mine detectors inaccurate. Marines and engineers were on their hands and knees in front of tanks, probing for mines with bayonets and wooden sticks.

While the 28th Marines battled to encircle Suribachi, the shore party and beachmasters struggled to clear the wreckage from the beaches. In the 5th Marine Division zone, the relatively fresh troops of the 1/26 and 3/27 Marines got bloodied. They forced their way across the western runways and took heavy casualties from time-fused airbursts and enemy dual-purpose antiaircraft guns. In the 4th Division zone, the 23rd Marines captured and secured the airstrip—advancing 800 yards with massive casualties.

Some of the most savage fighting was along the high ground above the Rock Quarry on the right flank. Here, the 25th Marines were engaged in the fight of their lives. Rifleman Richard Wheeler found the landscape, and the embedded enemy surreal: "there was no cover from enemy fire. Japs were in reinforced concrete pillboxes and laid down interlocking bands of fire that cut entire companies to pieces. Camouflage hid all their positions. The high ground on either side was honeycombed with layer after layer of Jap emplacements. They had a perfect observation of us. Whenever a Marine made a move, those damn Japs smothered the area with a murderous blanket of fire."

The second day of battle proved unacceptable on every front for the Marines. When the 1/24 Marines finally broke through along the cliffs late in the day, they were rewarded with back-to-back cases of friendly fire. A naval airstrike caused eleven casualties. Misguided salvos from an unidentified gunfire support ship took down another ninety troops. Nothing was going right.

The morning of D +2 promised more frustration. Marines shuddered in the chilly rain and wind. Admiral Hill twice closed the beach because of dangerous undertows and wicked surf. But during one of the grace periods, the 3/21 Marines came ashore, glad to be free of the heaving small boats.

The 20th Marines continued their attack on Suribachi's base. It was a slow, grinding, and bloody fight—boulder by boulder. On the western coast, the 1/28 Marines made the most of naval and field artillery gunfire support and reached the mountain's shoulder. Everywhere else, murderous enemy fire restricted any progress to a matter of yards. Enemy mortar fire from all over the volcano rained down on the 2/28 Marines, clawing their way along the eastern shore. Rifleman Richard Wheeler recalled: "it was terrible. Worst I can remember us ever taking. Jap mortar men played checkers with us as the squares."

The Marines used *Weasels*, handy tracked vehicles that made their first field appearance in this battle to hustle forward flamethrower canisters and evacuate the wounded. That night the amphibious task force experienced the only significant air attack of the battle. Forty-nine *kamikaze* pilots from the *22d Mitate Special Attack Unit* smashed into ships on the outer ring of Iwo Jima. In a desperate action, serving as a prelude to Okinawa's fiery hell, kamikaze pilots sank the escort carrier *Bismarck Sea* with heavy loss of life. They damaged several ships and knocked the veteran *Saratoga* out of the war. All forty-nine Japanese planes were destroyed.

On D +3, it rained even harder. Marines darted forward under fire, hitting the deck to return fire. They discovered that the loose volcanic sand, combined with rain, jammed their weapons. The 21st Marines at the vanguard ran headfirst into a series of enemy emplacements at the southeastern end of the Japanese defenses. Marines battled all day to scratch and claw and advance 200 yards. Casualties were disproportionate and horrific.

On the right flank, Colonel Chambers rallied the 3/25 Marines through the rough and rugged terrain above the Rock Quarry. While Chambers directed the advance of his decimated companies, an enemy sniper shot him in the chest. Chambers went down hard, thinking it was all over: "I faded in and out. I don't remember too much about it except a frothy blood gushing from my mouth. Then someone started kicking the hell out of my feet. It was Captain Headley yelling, 'get up, you were hurt worse on Tulagi.'"

Captain Headley knew Chamber's sucking chest wound was life-threatening. He tried to reduce his commander's shock until he could get him out of the line of fire. Lieutenant Mike Keller, the battalion surgeon, crawled forward with one of his corpsmen. They lifted Chambers onto a stretcher and through enemy fire, carried him down the cliffs to the aid station, and eventually onboard an amphibious truck to make the evening's last run out to the hospital ship. All three battalion commanders on the 25th Marines were now casualties. Chambers survived and received the Medal of Honor. Captain Headley took command of the shot-up 3/25th Marines for the rest of the fight.

The 20th Marines on D +3 made progress against Suribachi. They reached the shoulder on all points late in the day. Combat patrols from the 28th Marines linked up at Tobiishi Point: the southern tip of the island. Reconnaissance patrols reported they found few signs of life along the mountain's upper slopes and on the north side.

Admiral Spruance authorized Task Force 58 to strike Okinawa and Honshu at sundown. After that, they would go to Ulithi and prepare for the Ryukyuan campaign. All eight Marine Corps fighter squadrons left Iwo Jima for good. Navy pilots flying from the ten remaining escort carriers picked up the slack. While there was no question of the courage and skill of these pilots, the quality of close air support for the troops fighting ashore plummeted after the Marine fighter squadrons departed.

The escort carriers had too many other missions: combat air patrols, anti-submarine sweeps, downed pilot searches, and harassing strikes against neighboring Chichi Jima. Marines reported a slow response time for air support requests, light payloads, and high delivery altitudes. The navy pilots delivered several napalm bombs, but many failed to detonate. This wasn't the pilots' fault. The early napalm bombs were old wing-tanks filled with the mixture and activated by unreliable detonators. Marines on the ground were concerned about these notoriously inaccurate weapons being dropped from high altitudes.

On February 23, D +4, the 28th Marines were poised to capture Suribachi. This honor was given to Lieutenant Harry Schrier and Company E, 3rd Platoon. They were ordered to summit, secure the crater, and raise a 54" x 28" American flag for everyone to see. At 0800, Schrier led his forty-man patrol forward. The regiment had already blasted dozens of pillboxes with demolitions and flame. They'd rooted out snipers and knocked out the mass batteries. The combined arms hammering by planes, naval guns, and field pieces had finally taken their toll on the enemy. Any Japanese soldier who popped out of a cave to resist was cut to shreds. Marines carefully walked up the steep northern slope, sometimes resorting to crawling on hands and knees.

The Suribachi flag-raising drama has endured for so long because so many people observed it. All over the island,

Marines tracked the progress of the tiny column of troops during their ascent. Hundreds of binoculars from offshore ships watched Schrier's Marines climb. When they finally reached the top, they disappeared. Those closest to the volcano heard gunfire. Then at 1020, there was movement on the summit—the Stars & Stripes fluttered bravely in the breeze.

Cheers roared from the southern end of the island. Ships sounded sirens and whistles. Wounded men propped up on their litters to get a glimpse. Marines wept. Navy Secretary Forrestal was thrilled. He turned to General Holland Smith: "raising that flag means a Marine Corps for another five hundred years."

Three hours later, an even larger flag went up. Few knew that Associated Press photographer Joe Rosenthal had just captured the American war-fighting spirit on film. *Leatherneck* magazine Staff Sergeant Lou Lowery had taken a picture of the first flag raising and immediately got into a firefight with a handful of enraged enemy defenders. His photograph would become a valuable collector's item—but it was Rosenthal's that would enchant the free world.

Captain Tom Fields of Company D's 1/26 Marines heard his men yell: "Look up there!" and he turned in time to watch the first flag go up. His first thoughts were on the battle still at hand, and he remembered in the moment saying: "Thank God the Japs won't be shooting us down from behind anymore."

The 28th Marines captured and secured Mount Suribachi in three days at the cost of 900 casualties. Colonel Liversedge reoriented his regiment for operations to the north. Unknown to all, the battle of Iwo Jima still had another bloody thirty days before it would be over.

THE MEATGRINDER

It wasn't until the ninth day of battle that intelligence officers realized General Kuribayashi led the Japanese forces on Iwo Jima.

The unexpected early loss of the Suribachi garrison was a setback for Kuribayashi, but he still held a strong position. He had eight infantry battalions, two artillery and three heavy mortar battalions, and a tank regiment. Admiral Ichimaru had 5,000 naval infantry and gunners under his command, but unlike other besieged garrisons in the Central Pacific—these two Japanese leaders worked well together.

Kuribayashi was pleased with the quality of his artillery and engineering troops. His chief of artillery, Colonel Kaido, commanded from an impregnable concrete blockhouse in the east-central sector of the Motoyama Plateau. A lethal landmark the Marines called "Turkey Knob."

General Senda was an artillery officer with combat experience in Manchuria. He commanded the *2d Independent Mixed Brigade,* whose central units would be locked into a 25-day death struggle against the 4th Marine Division. The *204th Naval Construction Battalion* had built some of the most formidable defense systems on the island in his sector. One cave had an 800-foot-long tunnel with fourteen separate exits. It was only one of the hundreds defended to the bitter end.

Well-armed and confident enemy troops waited for the advance of the V Amphibious Corps. Kuribayashi ordered occasional company-sized attacks to recapture lost terrain or disrupt enemy assault preparations—but these were not sacrificial or suicidal. These mainly were preceded by stinging mortar and artillery fires and aimed at gaining limited objectives. General Kuribayashi's iron will kept his troops from large-scale, futile banzai attacks until the last few days.

An exception was on the evening of March 8. General

Senda, frustrated at the noose the 4th Division were applying, ordered 800 of his surviving troops into a ferocious counterattack. Finally, the Marines had targets out in the open. The suicidal Japanese attackers were cut to pieces with machine-gun and small arms fire.

For the first week of the drive north, the Japanese on Iwo had the assaulting Marines outgunned. The enemy's 120mm mortars and 150mm howitzers were superior to most of the weapons of the landing force. Marines found the enemy's direct fire weapons deadly. Especially the dual-purpose antiaircraft guns and the 47mm tank guns, buried up to their turrets. Retired General Donn Robertson said: "the Japs could snipe with those big guns. They also had the advantage of knowing the ground."

Most of the casualties in the first three weeks of battle were from high explosives: rocket bombs, grenades, mines, artillery, and hellacious mortars. Robert Sherrod (*Time* correspondent) wrote that the dead on Iwo Jima, both Japanese and Marine, had one thing in common: "they all died with the greatest possible violence. Nowhere in the Pacific War had I seen such badly mangled bodies. Many men were cut squarely in half."

The close combat was savage. Another constant stress for Marines was no secure rear area to put wounded troops. Kuribayashi's gunners hammered the beaches and airfields. Massive spigot mortar shells and rocket bombs tumbled from the sky. Japanese defenders were drawn to softer targets in the rear. Anti-personnel mines and booby-traps were everywhere and on a large scale for the first time in the Pacific.

Exhausted Marines stumbled out of the front line, seeking nothing more than a helmet full of water to bathe in and a deep hole to sleep in. Instead, Marines spent their rare rest repairing weapons, dodging incoming rounds, humping ammo, or having to repel another nighttime enemy probe.

General Schmidt planned to assault the northern Japanese positions with three divisions abreast. The 5th on the left, the 3rd in the center, and the 4th on the right. This northern drive would jump off on D +5: the day after securing Mount Suribachi. Preparatory fires along the high ground north of the second airfield would last for an hour. Then three regimental combat teams would advance abreast: 26th Marines on the left, 24th on the right, and the 21st in the center. For this assault, Schmidt merged all three divisions' Sherman tanks into one armor task force—commanded by Colonel "Rip" Collins. This would be the largest concentration of Marine tanks in the Pacific War: an armored regiment.

Marines recognized they were trying to force a passage

through Kuribayashi's primary defensive belt. The assault deteriorated into multiple desperate small unit actions along the front. While the 26th Marines (with the help of tanks) gained the most yards, it was still relative. Airfield runways were lethal killing zones. Mines and high-velocity direct fire destroyed Sherman tanks all along the front. On the right flank, Colonel Alexander Vandegrift (son of Marine Commandant Alexander Vandegrift) was wounded.

During the fighting on D +5, General Schmidt moved his command post onshore from the amphibious force flagship *Auburn*. Schmidt now had eight entire infantry regiments committed to the battle. General Holland Smith still had the 3rd Marines and expeditionary troops in reserve. Schmidt made his first of multiple requests to Smith to release that seasoned outfit. The V Amphibious Corps had already taken 6,845 casualtics.

On February 25, D +6, enemy resistance intensified. Small Marine units escorted by tanks made progress along the runway. Each Marine was under the impression he was alone in the middle of a giant bowling alley. Often, holding newly gained positions across the runway proved more deadly than capturing them. Resupplying the troops became virtually impossible. Precious Sherman tanks were getting destroyed at an alarming rate.

General Schmidt got two battalions of 105mm howitzers ashore under the command of Colonel John Letcher. Well-directed fire from these heavy field pieces eased some of the pressure on the assaulting Marines. While fire from destroyers and cruisers was marginally effective, air support was a total disappointment. The 3rd Marine Division later complained that the Navy's assignment of eight fighters and eight bombers on station was utterly inadequate.

At noon, General Cates sent a message to Schmidt requesting the strategic Air Force in the Marianas immediately replace Navy air support. Colonel McGee, air commander on Iwo, took heat from the frustrated division commanders. He later wrote: "those little spit kit Navy fighters up there were trying to help but were never enough and were never where they needed to be."

In fairness, it's debatable if any service could have provided adequate air support within the opening days of the northern drive. The air liaison parties within each regiment played hell trying to identify and mark targets. The enemy kept a masterful camouflage. Japanese frontline units were often eyeball to eyeball with Marines, and the air support request net was often overloaded.

Navy squadrons flying from the decks of escort carriers eventually improved by adding heavier bombs and improving their response times. A week later, General Cates rated his air support as satisfactory. But the battle of Iwo Jima would continue to frustrate Allied forces; the Japanese never assembled legitimate targets in the open. Captain Fields of the 26th Marines wrote after the war: "the Japs weren't *on* Iwo Jima. They were *in* Iwo Jima."

Richard Wheeler, who survived Iwo Jima with the 28th Marines, wrote two books about the battle. "This was one of the strangest battlefields in history. One side fought wholly above ground, and the other operated within it. During the battle, American aerial observers marveled that one side of the field had thousands of figures milling around or in foxholes while the other side was deserted. But the strangest of all was that the two contestants sometimes made troop movements simultaneously in the same territory with one maneuvering on the surface and the other using tunnels below."

As the Marines fought like hell to capture the second

airfield from the Japanese, the terrain features rising to the north caught their attention. While there were three hills named 362 on the island, Marines had different nicknames for them: "Amphitheater" and "Turkey Knob." But the bristling complex of hills and terrain would be forever known as "The Meatgrinder."

The 5th Marine Division earned their spurs and lost many of their precious veteran leaders fighting on "The Gorge" and attacking Nishi Ridge (Hills 362-A and B).

The 3rd Marine Division focused their assault north of the second airfield and then onto the heavily fortified Hill 362-C beyond the airstrip. Finally, they attacked the moonscape jungle of stone, soon to be known as "Cushman's pocket."

Colonel Robert Cushman commanded the 2/9 Marines on Iwo. Cushman and his Marines were veterans of heavy fighting on Guam but were stunned by their first sight of the battlefield. Burned out and smoldering Sherman tanks dotted airstrips. Casualties streamed to the rear. The terrific and horrific echo of machine-gun fire was everywhere. Cushman mounted his troops on the surviving tanks and rumbled across the field. They met the same reverse-slope defenses that dogged the 21st Marines. But after three days of savage fighting, Cushman's Marines secured the two Hills north of the second airfield, Peter and 199-Oboe.

General Schmidt made the 3rd Division attack in the center of his main effort. He gave the 3rd priority fire support from the corps artillery. He directed the other two divisions to allocate half of their regimental fire support to the center. The other commanders were not pleased. Neither the 4th Marine Division, who took heavy casualties in the Amphitheater, nor the 5th Division, who struggled to seize Nishi Ridge, wanted to dilute their organic fire support.

General Graves Erskine argued the main effort should

receive the primary fire. Schmidt never solved this problem. His corps artillery was too late, and he needed twice as many battalions and bigger guns: the 8-inch howitzers, which the Marines had not yet fielded. Schmidt had plenty of naval gunfire support available and used it abundantly. But unless targets were in ravines facing the sea—he lost the advantage of observed direct fire.

General Schmidt's fire support problems were eased on February 26. Two Marine observation planes flew in from the carrier *Wake Island* and were the first planes to land on Iwo's recently recaptured, fire swept main airstrip. These were single-engine observation planes (Grasshoppers). They were followed the next day by similar planes from VMO-5. The pilots of these fragile planes had already had an exciting time in the waters off Iwo. Many were launched from the experimental catapult on *LST-776*: "like a peanut from a slingshot."

All fourteen of these observation planes took heavy enemy fire airborne and while serviced on the airstrips. But these two squadrons flew 612 missions supporting all three divisions. Few units contributed as much to the eventual suppression of Kuribayashi's murderous artillery fire. The mere presence of the small planes overhead caused Japanese gunners to cease fire and button-up against the inevitable counter-battery fire soon to follow. Grasshopper pilots would fly predawn or dust missions to extend a protective umbrella over the troops. This was risky flying because of Iwo's unlit fields and snipers hidden in the hills.

When the 4th Marine Division finally secured Hill 382 at the highest point north of Suribachi, they still suffered heavy casualties moving through the Amphitheater against Turkey knob. The 5th Marine Division seized Nishi Ridge and bloodied themselves on Hill 362-A's elaborate defenses.

Colonel Tom Wornham, CO, 27th Marines: "they had interlocking fields of fire the likes of which I'd never seen before."

General Cates redeployed the 28th Marines into the fight. On March 2, an enemy gunner fired a high-velocity shell that killed Colonel Chandler Johnson one week after his glorious seizure of the Suribachi Summit. The 28th Marines captured Hill 362-A—at the cost of 200 casualties.

The same day, Colonel Lowell English, CO 2/21 Marines, took a bullet in his knee. Colonel English was upset that his battalion was not rotating to the rear: "We took heavy casualties and were disorganized. I had less than 300 Marines left of the 1,200 I came ashore with." Colonel English received orders to turn his Marines around and plug a gap in the front lines. "It was an impossible order. I couldn't move that disorganized battalion a mile back to the north in thirty minutes."

But General Erskine did not want excuses: "tell that *Goddamned* English he'd better be there."

Colonel English replied: "you tell that son of a bitch I will be there, and I was, but my men were still half a mile behind me, and I got a hole in my knee!"

The 26th Marines fought their bloodiest and most successful attack of the battle on the left flank—finally securing Hill 362-B. This all-day battle cost 500 Marine casualties and produced five Medals of Honor. For Captain Frank Caldwell of Company F, 1/26 Marines, it was the worst day of his life. His company took forty-nine casualties on that hill—as well as the first sergeant and all the original platoon commanders.

The first nine days of the V Amphibious Corps' northern drive produced a net gain of only 4,000 yards at a horrific cost of 7,000 Marine casualties. Several of these pitched battles in The Meatgrinder would've been worthy of a separate book. The fighting was one of the most brutal and bloody in the Marine Corps' history.

On D +13, March 4, came the turning point. After alarming and frightful losses, Marines had torn through a substantial chunk of General Kuribayashi's primary defenses. Forcing the enemy commander to shift his command post to a northern cave. On this afternoon, the first crippled B-29 landed. In terms of Allied morale, it couldn't have come at a better time. General Schmidt ordered a standdown on March 5 to enable the exhausted assault forces a brief rest and the opportunity to absorb replacements.

The issue of replacement troops throughout this battle is controversial—even seventy-seven years later. General Schmidt had suffered losses approaching the equivalent of an entire division (6,561 Marines). Schmidt urged Holland Smith to release the 3rd Marines. While each division had been assigned several thousand Marine replacements, Schmidt wanted the cohesion and combat experience of Colonel Jim Stewart's regimental combat team. Holland Smith argued the replacements would suffice and believed that each replacement Marine in these hybrid units had received sufficient infantry training to fulfill immediate assignment to the frontline outfits.

The next challenge was distributing the replacements in small arbitrary numbers—not teamed units—to plug the gaping holes in the assault battalions. These new men were expected to replace the vital veterans of the Pacific War. These replacement Marines were not only new to combat but also to each other—an assortment of strangers that lacked the life-saving bonds of unit integrity.

One frustrated Marine officer said: "they get killed the day they go into battle." Losses among the replacement Marines within the first forty-eight hours of combat were shocking. Those who survived and learned the ropes established a bond with the veterans and contributed significantly to the battle's victory. Division commanders criticized the wastefulness of this policy and urged for replacements from the veteran battalions of the 3rd Marines.

General Erskine later wrote: "I asked Kelly Turner and Holland Smith to give us the 3rd. They said, 'you got enough Marines on the island now. There are too damn many here already.' I said, 'this is an easy solution. Some of these Marines are tired and too worn out, so take them out and bring in the goddamn 3rd Marines.' They said, 'keep your mouth shut. We made our decision.' And that was that."

Most surviving officers agreed that the decision not to use the veteran 3rd Marines at Iwo was wasteful and ill-advised. But Holland Smith never wavered: "sufficient troops were on Iwo Jima for the capture of the island. Two regiments were sufficient to cover the frontal assault assigned to General Erskine."

On D +14, March 5, General Holland Smith ordered the 3rd Marines to sail back to Guam.

* * *

While Holland Smith may have known the overall statistics of the battle losses sustained by the landing force at that point—he did not fully appreciate the tremendous attrition of experienced junior officers and senior noncoms taking their place every day. For example, the day after the 3rd Marines sailed for Guam, the 2/23 Marines' E Company suffered the loss of their seventh company commander since the start of the battle.

Colonel Cushman's experiences with the 2/9 Marines were typical: "casualties were brutal. By the time Iwo was over, we'd gone through two complete sets of lieutenants and platoon leaders. After that, we had forward artillery observers commanding companies and sergeants leading half strength platoons. It was that bad."

Colonel English wrote: "After twelve days, we'd lost every company commander. I had one company exec left. I'd lost all three of my rifle company commanders killed by the same damn shell."

Many infantry units and platoons ceased to exist. Depleted companies were merged to form half-strength outfits.

NORTHERN ALLIED DRIVE

The Allied drive continued north after the March 5 stand-down. It did not get any easier. The Japanese had changed tactics: fewer big guns and rockets and less observed fire from the highlands. But now, the terrain had deteriorated into narrow gorges, enveloped in sulfur mists—killing zones.

Allied casualties mounted. Gunshot wounds now outnumbered the high explosive shrapnel hits. A myth among Marine units was that the Japanese were nearsighted and poor marksmen. In close quarters fighting in northern Iwo, Japanese riflemen shot down hundreds of advancing Marines in the head or chest with well-aimed fire. Captain Caldwell of the 1/26 Marines said: "Poor marksmen? All the Japs we faced were expert shooters."

Supporting arms coordination became more effective during the battle. Colonel "Buzz" Letcher established the first SACC (Supporting Arms Coordination Center), where senior artillery, naval gunfire, and air support representatives pooled their talents and resources. While Letcher lacked the manpower and communications equipment to run a full-time SACC, his efforts significantly advanced this challenging art.

Colonel McGee's Landing Force Air Support Control Unit worked in harmony with the fledgling SACC. Still, friendly fire incidents happened. Perhaps friendly fire was inevitable on that crowded island, but positive control at the highest level did much to reduce the frequency of these accidents.

The lack of preliminary naval bombardment on Iwo angered Marines. While all hands valued the responsive support received from D-Day onward, the lack of initial fire was blamed for the horrific Marine casualties. The gunfire ships stood in close—less than a mile offshore—and hammered the flanks and front lines. Many ships took hits from the hidden enemy coastal defense batteries. There were no safe zones in or around Iwo Jima.

Two characteristics of naval gunfire on Iwo were notable: The extent ships provided illuminating rounds over the battlefield, especially during the early days before the landing force artillery could assume the bulk of these missions. Second was the degree of assistance provided by the smaller gunships, frequently modified with 4.2-inch mortars, 20mm guns, or rockets. These "small boys" were vital along the northwestern coast as they worked in lockstep with the 5th Marine Division advancing toward The Gorge.

While the Marines comprised most of the landing force on Iwo, they still received support from the army. Two of the four amphibious truck companies on D-Day were army units. The 138th Antiaircraft Artillery Group placed their 90mm batteries around the newly captured airfields. General Jim Chaney (later to become Iwo's island commander) landed on D +8 with elements of the Army's 145th Infantry.

Army units flew into Iwo on March 6 (D +15). The 15th Fighter Group arrived to escort B-29s over Tokyo. This group was a seasoned outfit that included the famous 47th Fighter Squadron and their P-51 Mustangs. While the army pilots had little to no experience in direct air support of ground troops, Colonel McGee was impressed with their "eager beaver attitude" and willingness to learn.

McGee appreciated the fact the Mustangs could deliver thousand-pound bombs. He had the Army pilots trained on how to strike designated targets on nearby islands. In three days, they were ready for duty on Iwo. McGee instructed the Mustang pilots to arm their bombs with twelve-second delay fuses and attack parallel to the front lines approaching from a 45° angle.

These tactics often produced stunning results—especially along the west coast—where the thousand-pound bombs blew sides of entire cliffs off into the ocean. This exposed enemy caves and tunnels to direct naval gunfire from the sea. According to McGee: "those Air Force boys did a lot of good."

The field medical support given to the assaulting Marines

was a major contributor to victory on Iwo. Integrating chaplains, surgeons, and corpsmen within the FMF (Fleet Marine Force) paid valuable dividends. Most times, corpsmen were as tough and combat savvy as the Marines in that company. Wounded Marines knew their corpsman would move heaven and earth to reach them, bind their wounds, and start the long evacuation process.

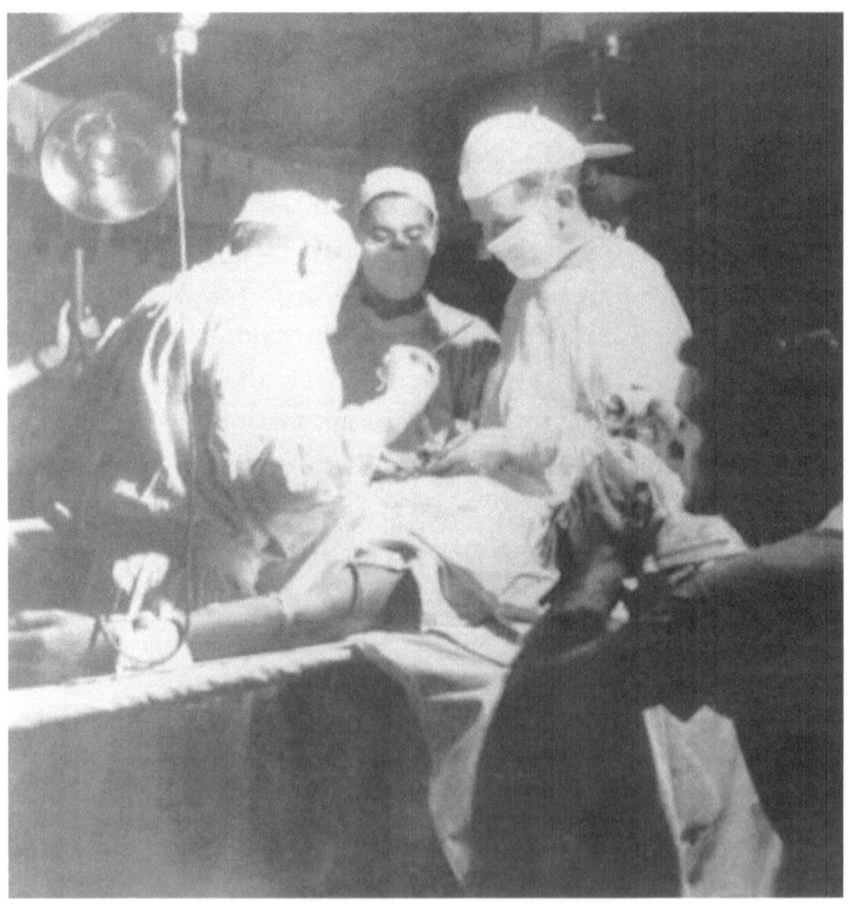

Marines on Iwo Jima echoed the views of Staff Sergeant Al Thomas: "we had outstanding corpsmen. They were our family." The luxury of having first-rate medical help so close to the front took a terrible toll. Eight hundred twenty-seven corpsmen and twenty-three doctors were wounded or killed on Iwo Jima—a casualty rate twice as high as Saipan.

Combat medical support was thoughtfully prepared and provided on Iwo. Past the crude aid stations and toward the rear, the Army and Navy field hospitals arose. Wounded Marines would receive treatment in a field hospital, then recuperate in a bunker before returning to the lines to often receive their second or third wound. The more seriously wounded were evacuated by air to Guam or to one of the several fully-staffed hospital ships operating around the clock. Within the first month of fighting on Iwo, 13,747 Marines and corpsmen casualties were evacuated by hospital ship and another 2,489 by airlift.

When a Marine was wounded, the first few minutes were the most dangerous after going down. Enemy snipers had no hesitations about picking off corpsmen, litter crews, or even the wounded man himself as his buddies tried to slide him out of the fire.

Corporal Ed Canter was a rocket truck crew chief in the 4th Marine Division. Rocket trucks always drew an angry barrage of counter-battery fire from the enemy. A Japanese sniper shot Canter through the stomach. Corporal Canter's comrades knew they had to get him away from that launch site fast. As a nearby motion picture crew recorded the drama, four Marines carried Canter down a mud-covered hillside. They heard the scream of an incoming shell and dumped Canter while they took cover.

The explosion killed the film crew and wounded each of the Marines, including Canter again. The film footage survived and appeared in US newsreels—before becoming a part of the movie *Sands of Iwo Jima*. Corporal Canter survived and was evacuated to a hospital ship and then to different hospitals in Guam and Hawaii before returning to the US. His war was over.

* * *

The shore party personnel and beachmasters performed remarkable feats of logistics to keep the advancing divisions equipped and armed. The logistical management and sheer backbreaking work needed to maintain such a high volume of supplies and equipment moving over these dangerous beaches was hard to imagine. A single beach on the west coast became functional on D +11, but by that time, most of the landing force supplies were already ashore.

The next day after the general unloading was completed, the vulnerable amphibious ships were released from their tether to the beachhead. Shortly after, well-aimed enemy fire detonated the 5th Marine Division's entire ammo dump. Ammunition resupply became vital. Then, the ammunition ship *Columbia Victory* came under direct enemy fire as she approached the western beaches to unload. Waiting Marines held their breath as the *Columbia Victory* was nearly destroyed. She narrowly escaped, but the potential for disaster still loomed.

An entire brigade of the 62nd Naval Construction Battalion (Seabees) extended and repaired the captured runways. Marines returning to the beaches from the northern highlands could scarcely recognize the place they'd first seen on D-Day. There were now over 80,000 Allied troops on the small island, and the Seabees had bulldozed a two-lane road to the top of Mount Suribachi.

Communications had improved dramatically on Iwo compared to previous amphibious campaigns. Handsets and radios were now waterproof and had more frequencies.

Forward observer teams used the backpack SCR-610, while companies and platoons preferred the walkie-talkie style SCR-300 or even lighter portables, the "Spam Can" SCR-536.

Colonel Jim Berkeley, XO of the 27th Marines said: "On Iwo, we had near-perfect communications. It was all any commander could ask for." Marines strung telephone lines between support units and four command posts as the battle raged, elevating the wire along upright posts to avoid damage by tracked vehicles.

Enemy counterintelligence expected to have an easy day splicing into allied phone lines, but Marines baffled them with Navajo code talkers. Each division employed twenty-four trained Navajos. The 5th Marine Division's command post had six established Navajo networks on the island. No one throughout the war could ever crack the Navajo code.

Black American troops played a major role in the capture of Iwo. Black troops drove army amphibious trucks and were active throughout the landing. Black Marines of the 8th Ammunition Company and the 36th Depot Company landed on D-Day and served as longshoremen on those chaotic, bloody beaches. The on-island Black Marines worked with the Shore Party and helped to sustain the momentum of the Allied northern drive. When the Japanese counterattacked penetrated these beach areas, Black Marines dropped their cargo, unslung their carbines, and engaged the enemy with well-disciplined fire.

Colonel Leland Swindler commanded the V Amphibious Corps Shore Party: "the entire body of Black Marines under my command conducted themselves with marked coolness and courage and inflicted more casualties on the enemy than they sustained."

News coverage of the Iwo Jima battle was extensive. Dozens of combat correspondents were embedded with the landing force throughout the battle. Marine Sergeant "Dick" Dashiell was a writer for the Associated Press and assigned to the 3rd Marine Division. Although sometimes terrified and filled with horror, Dashiell endured and wrote eighty-one frontline stories and pounded out news releases on his portable typewriter at the edge of his foxhole. Dashiell's eye for detail always caught the attention of the reader: "All is bitter. Frontal assault always uphill. A ceaseless wind filled the air with a fine volcanic grit." He described how Marines had to stop and clean the grit from their weapons—and how naked that made most Marines feel.

Occasionally, hot food was delivered to the exhausted Marines on the front lines. The deliveries of milk and fruit from nearby ships boosted morale. So did watching the crippled B-29s zoom in for an emergency landing. Sergeant "Doc" Lindsey was a squad leader in Company G, 2/25 Marines. He stated: "It was good to see them land. You knew they'd just come from hitting Tokyo."

DEFIANT TO THE END

General Erskine caught pneumonia but refused to evacuate. His Chief of Staff, Colonel Robert Hogaboom, kept the war moving behind the scenes. The division continued its advance, and when Erskine recovered—Hogaboom adjusted accordingly. The two were an effective team.

Erskine had long wanted to conduct a battalion-size night operation. It bothered him that throughout the war, the Allies had yielded the night to the Japanese. When Hill 362-C continued to thwart his advance, Erskine ordered a predawn assault without the trappings of preparatory fire, which always identified the time and place of attack.

The honor of leading this unusual attack was put to Colonel "Bing" Boehm, CO, 3/9 Marines. But this battalion was new to the sector and received their attack order too late to reconnoiter effectively. Absent of advance orientation, the battalion crossed the line of departure silently at 0500 and advanced toward Hill 362-C. The unit achieved total surprise. Before the sleepy Japanese knew it, the Marines swept across 500 yards of broken ground and roasted enemy outposts and strong points with flamethrowers.

When daylight revealed that Boehm's battalion had captured the wrong hill (Hill 362-C was still 250 yards distant), his battalion was surrounded by a sea of furious and wide-awake and counterattacking enemy infantry. Boehm redeployed his battalion and attacked toward the original hill. This was rough going and took most of the day, but before dark, the 3/9 Marines secured Hill 362-C—a main Japanese defensive anchor.

The Allied positions grew stronger after General Senda's counterattack against the 4th Marine Division. On D +18, a patrol from the 3rd Marine Division reached the northeast coast. The squad leader filled his canteen with saltwater and sent it to General Schmidt marked: "For Inspection, Not Consumption."

Schmidt welcomed the symbolism. The next day, the 4th Marine Division finally secured Turkey Knob and advanced toward The Amphitheater on the east coast. While the end was in sight, the intensity of the Japanese resistance did not fade. In the 5th Division's western zone, the 2/26 reported a casualty rate of seventy percent. General Keller Rockey reported his Marines were: "in a state of extreme fatigue and exhaustion."

Division commanders looked to relieve their shot-up men. General Cates formed a provisional battalion in the 4th Marine Division under Colonel Melvin Krulewitch. He was ordered to attack bypassed enemy positions. While the term "mopping up" was used, it was considered inaccurate by many Allied troops. Countless pockets of Japanese held out—defiant and well-armed to the end. Rooting them out was never easy. Marines used pioneers, motor transport units, and amtracs, as light infantry units to strengthen frontline battalions and conduct combat patrols.

In the extreme rear on Iwo Jima, the men had become overconfident. Movies were shown every night and ice cream could be found on the beach. Men swam in the surf and slept in tents in a deadly and false sense of security.

To the north, Colonel Cushman's 2/9 Marines were engaged in broken terrain east of the airfield. Marines ultimately encircled the enemy's position, but the battle of "Cushman's Pocket," raged on. Cushman's battalion commander reported the action: "The Jap position is a maze of pillboxes, caves, emplaced tanks, stonewalls, and trenches. We beat against them for eight continuous days using every support weapon. Our core objective in the sector still remains. Our battalion is exhausted, and most of our leaders are gone. Our battalion now numbers 387 with 350 replacements."

Cushman's 2/9 was ultimately relieved by elements of the 9th and 21st Marines (equally exhausted) and had just as difficult of a time. General Erskine had no reserves. He ordered Cushman back into the pocket, and by March 16, (D +25) enemy resistance in the thicket of jumbled rocks ended.

* * *

The 4th Marine Division poured over the hills in the east and secured the coastal road by blasting the last Japanese strong points from the rear. Ninety percent of Iwo Jima was in Allied hands. Radio Tokyo announced the fall of Iwo Jima as: "the most unfortunate thing in the whole war situation."

General Holland Smith took the opportunity to declare victory and conduct a flag-raising ceremony. Following that, the old warhorse departed along with Admiral Kelly Turner. Now, General Schmidt and Admiral Hill finally had the campaign to themselves. Survivors of the 4th Marine Division began backloading on board ship—their battle finally over.

The killing continued in the north. The 5th Marine Division entered The Gorge, an 800-yard pocket of broken country the troops called "Death Valley." General Kuribayashi would make his last stand here in a command center in a deep cave. Fighting through this horrid moonscape was a fitting end to the battle—nine days of cave-by-cave assaults with demolitions and flamethrowers. Marine combat engineers used 9,000 tons of explosives to detonate one massive fortification. Progress was bloody and slow. General Rockey's depleted and drained regiments lost one man for every two yards gained. General Schmidt deployed the 3rd Division against Kitano Point in the 5th Division zone to ease the pressure.

Colonel Hartnoll Withers led the final assault with the 21st Marines against the extreme northern tip of the island. General Erskine's pneumonia be damned. He came along to look over Withers' shoulder. The 21st Marines felt the end was near. Their momentum was irresistible. In a few hours of sharp fighting, they cleared out the last of the resistance. Erskine signaled Schmidt: "Kitano Point Taken."

Allied forces tried to persuade Kuribayashi to surrender during these last days. They broadcasted appeals in Japanese and sent him personal messages, praising his bravery, and urging his cooperation. General Kuribayashi was a samurai to the end. In his last message to Tokyo: "We have not eaten or drank for five days, but our fighting spirit is still running high. We will fight to the end for our Emperor."

Imperial Headquarters tried to convey the good news that the emperor had approved his promotion to full general. There was no response from Iwo Jima. It would be a posthumous promotion. Controversial Japanese evidence revealed that he committed *Seppuku* on the night of March 25.

The 5th Marine Division clawed their way forward in The Gorge. The average battalion that landed with thirty-six officers and 885 men on D-Day now only had sixteen officers and 300 men. This included the hundreds of replacements funneled in through the battle. Remnants of the 1/26 and 1/28 Marines squeezed the enemy into a final pocket and destroyed them.

On the evening of March 25 (D +34), the battle for Iwo Jima was over. The island became eerily quiet. Far fewer illumination shells flickered a false light on the shadowy figures moving south toward the airfield. General Schmidt got the good news that the 5th Marine Division had snuffed out the last enemy cave. As the corps commander prepared to declare the end of organized resistance on Iwo Jima—a well-organized enemy force emerged from the northern caves and snuck down the length of the island.

This last spasm of Japanese resistance reflected the enemy's tactical discipline. A 300-man Japanese force took all night to move into position around the island's vulnerable rear area. Newly arrived army pilots from the VII Fighter Command were surprised in their tents. The enemy force attacked the sleeping pilots with grenades, swords, and automatic rifles. The fighting was as savage and bloody as any on Iwo Jima.

Men from the 5th Pioneer Battalion and surviving pilots formed a skirmish line and launched a counterattack. Seabees and redeploying 28th Marines joined the fight. There were few suicides among the Japanese. Most died in battle. Grateful to strike one final blow for their emperor. Sunrise uncovered the carnage—300 dead enemy and over a hundred slaughtered pilots, Seabees, and pioneers along with another 200 wounded. It was a grotesque closing chapter to five savage weeks of killing and carnage.

LEGACY OF IWO JIMA

In thirty-six days of combat, the V Amphibious Corps killed nearly 22,000 Japanese sailors and soldiers. This was achieved at a staggering cost. Marine assault units (along with organic Navy personnel) suffered 24,053 casualties—6,140 killed—the highest single action losses in Marine Corps history. Statistically, for every three Marines who landed on Iwo Jima, one became a casualty.

According to military historian Norman Cooper: "Seven hundred Americans gave their lives for every square mile. For every plot of ground the size of a football field, an average of one American and five Japanese were killed, and five Americans wounded."

Assault units bore the brunt of these casualties. Captain Bill Ketcham's Company I, 3/24 Marines, landed on D-Day with 133 Marines and three rifle platoons. Only nine of these men remained when his company re-embarked on D +35.

Captain Frank Caldwell reported a loss of 220 men from Company F, 1/26 Marines. By the end, a private first class commanded a platoon in Captain Caldwell's merged 1st and 2nd Platoons.

Captain Tom Fields relinquished command of Company D on the eighth day to replace his battalion's executive officer. When he rejoined his company at the end of the battle, Fields was sickened to find only seventeen of the original 250 Marines still alive.

Company B of the 1/28 Marines went through nine company commanders in the fight. Twelve different Marines served as platoon leaders of the 2nd Platoon—including two buck privates. Other divisions reported similar conditions.

The American public reacted with shock and sadness as they had fourteen months earlier on Tarawa. The debate about the high cost of forcibly seizing an enemy island raged in the press while the battle was being fought. The Marine Corps released only one statement on February 22 about detailed battle losses during the fighting. They reported casualties of nearly 5,000.

William Randolph Hearst was an early supporter of the MacArthur for President campaign. Hearst ran a front-page editorial in the *San Francisco Examiner* blaming the horrific Marine losses on poor tactics: "it's the same thing that happened on Saipan and Tarawa." The editorial urged for the elevation of General MacArthur to supreme commander of the Pacific: "HE SAVES THE LIVES OF HIS OWN MEN."

One hundred off-duty Marines disagreed and stormed the offices of the examiner and demanded an apology. But the Hearst editorial had already received wide play. Many families of men fighting in the Pacific were forwarded the clippings. Marines received these in the mail while the fighting still raged on Iwo—an unwelcome blow for morale.

FDR, an expert in manipulating public opinion, kept a lid on the outcry by emphasizing the troops' sacrifice as symbolized by Joe Rosenthal's Suribachi flag-raising. While this photograph was already famous, Roosevelt made it the official logo of the Seventh War Bond Drive. He ordered the six flag raisers be reassigned home to boost morale, but three out of those six men had already been killed in the fighting on Iwo Jima.

The Joint Chiefs studied Iwo's losses. No one questioned the objective: Iwo Jima was an island that had to be secured to launch an effective strategic bombing campaign. The island could not have been bypassed or leapfrogged. There was evidence the Joint Chiefs considered using poison gas during the planning phase. Neither the US nor Japan had signed the international cessation on poison gas, and there were no civilians on the island. The US had stockpiled mustard gas shells in the Pacific Theater. When FDR read the report, he shot down the idea. He publicly stated that the United States would never make *first use* of poison gas. This left the landing force with no other option but a frontal amphibious assault against the most heavily fortified island the United States had ever faced.

The capture of Iwo Jima provided other strategic and symbolic benefits. Marines raised the flag over Suribachi the same day MacArthur entered Manila. The parallel captures of the Philippines and Suribachi were followed immediately by the invasion of Okinawa—accelerating the pace of the war and bringing it at long last to Japan's doorstep. These three campaigns proved to the Japanese command that the Allies had the capability and will to overwhelm even the most resolutely defended islands. Honshu and Kyushu would be next.

The capture of Iwo Jima delivered immediate benefits to the strategic bombing campaign. Marines fighting on the island were reminded of this mission repeatedly as crippled B-29s flew in from Honshu. Securing and rebuilding Iwo's airfields increased the operating range payload and survival rate of the big bombers. The monthly tonnage of high explosives dropped on Japan by the B-29s based in the Marianas increased eleven-fold in March alone. On April 7, eighty P-51 Mustangs took off from Iwo, escorting the B-29s bombing the Nakajima aircraft engine plant in Tokyo.

The great value of Iwo's airfields was that they could be used as emergency landing fields. By war's end, 2,252 B-29s made forced landings on Iwo. These forced landings included 24,765 flight crewmen. Many of these men would have perished at sea without Iwo's safe haven. According to one B-29 pilot: "whenever I landed on that island, I thanked God for the men who fought and died for it."

General Kuribayashi proved to be one of the most competent field commanders the Marines had ever faced. His expert understanding of simplicity and economy of force made maximum use of Iwo's formidable terrain. He deployed his mortars and artillery with great skill and commanded his troops with an iron will—to the end. He was a realist. With no hope of naval or air superiority, he knew he was doomed from the start. Allied forces took five weeks to breach every strong point and exterminate his forces on the island.

Iwo Jima was the pinnacle of Allied amphibious capabilities in the Pacific. The sheer magnitude of planning the assault and sustaining the landing forces made Operation Detachment an enduring model of detailed planning and violent execution. The element of surprise was not available. But the speed of the landing force and the toughness with which assault units withstood the withering barrages amazed the enemy defenders.

Colonel Wornham of the 27th Marines said: "The Iwo landing was the epitome of everything we'd learned over the years about amphibious assaults. Bad as the enemy fire was on D-Day, there were no reports of 'Issue in doubt.'"

Colonel Galer compared his Guadalcanal experience to the battle on Iwo: "then, it was can we hold? On Iwo, the question was simply, when can we get this over?"

While the ship-to-shore assaults were impressive, the actual degree of amphibious effectiveness was seen in the massive, sustained logistical support which flowed over the treacherous beaches. Marines had all the ammunition and flamethrower refills they needed around the clock. They also had many less obvious necessities that marked this battle differently than its predecessors. Marines on Iwo had enough quantities of whole blood, most donated two weeks in advance, flown in, refrigerated, and always available.

Marines had mail call, clean water, radio batteries, fresh-baked bread, and prefabricated burial markers. The Iwo Jima operation was a model of interservice cooperation. Marine and Navy teams functioned efficiently together. The Navy earned the respect of the Marines on D -2 when a flotilla of tiny LCI gunboats fearlessly attacked the coastal defense guns to protect the Navy and Marine frogmen. Marines appreciated the contributions of the Coast Guard, Army, Red Cross, and embedded combat correspondents; all shared in the misery and glory of this battle.

The US Military occupied Iwo Jima until 1968, when jurisdiction was transferred back to Japan. Seventy-seven years later, the island remains a military-only island. It is no longer a baren moonscape, but covered in rich greenery, yet two aspects of this battle are still controversial: inadequate preliminary bombardment and the decision to use piecemeal replacements instead of organized units to strengthen the assault forces. Both decisions were made in the context of several competing factors and were made by experienced commanders in good faith. Iwo Jima's highest cost was the loss of so many combat veterans while taking the island. While this battle created a new generation of veteran heroes among the survivors, many proud regiments suffered devastating losses.

Those veteran regiments had already been designated as crucial landing force components in the Japanese home islands assault—these losses had severe potential implications. It may have been these factors that influenced Holland Smith's unpopular decision to withhold the 3rd Marines from the battle.

To many exhausted Marines and commanders fighting on Iwo Jima, Holland Smith's decision to withhold the 3rd Marines was unforgivable—then and now. But whatever his flaws, General Holland Smith almost certainly knew amphibious warfare better than anyone at the time.

According to Holland Smith: "We had no hope of surprise, either tactical or strategic. There was little possibility for tactical initiative. The entire operation was fought on virtually the enemy's terms. The strength, conduct, and disposition of the enemy's defense required a major penetration of his prepared positions in the center of the Motoyama Plateau and a subsequent reduction of his positions in rugged terrain sloping to the shore on the flanks.

"The terrain and size of the island precluded any Force Beachhead Line. It was a one-phase and one-tactic operation. From the time the engagement was joined until the mission was completed, it was a frontal assault maintained with relentless pressure by a superior force in supporting arms against a position fortified to the maximum practical intent.

"We Americans of a subsequent generation in the profession of arms find it difficult to imagine a sustained amphibious assault under these conditions. In some respects, the fighting on Iwo Jima took the features of the Marines fighting in France in 1918. We sensed the drama repeated every morning on Iwo Jima after the prep fires lifted, when the rifleman, engineers, corpsman, flame tank crews, and armored bulldozers somehow found the fortitude to move out again into The Meatgrinder or Death Valley. Few of us today can study the defenses, analyze the after-action reports, or walk that broken ground without experiencing a sense of reverence for the men who fought and won that epic battle."

While the fighting was raging on Iwo, Admiral Nimitz said: "Among the Americans serving on Iwo Jima, uncommon valor was a common virtue." This line was chiseled into the base of Felix de Weldon's giant bronze sculpture of the Suribachi flag-raising.

On Iwo, Twenty-two Marines, four Navy corpsmen, and one LCI skipper were awarded the Medal of Honor for bravery during the battle—half were awarded posthumously.

General Erskine put the Allied sacrifices into perspective during his remarks at the dedication of the 3rd Marine Division's Cemetery on Iwo Jima: "Our victory was never in doubt. Its cost was. What was in doubt, in all of our minds, was whether there would be any of us left to dedicate this cemetery at the end. Or if the last Marine would die knocking out the last Japanese gunner."

ICONIC FLAG RAISING

There were two flags raised over Mount Suribachi—but not at the same time. On the morning of February 23, 1945, (D +4)

Captain Dave Severance, Company E Commander, 2/28 Marines, ordered Lieutenant Harold Schrier to take a patrol and put up an American flag on the top of Mount Suribachi.

Staff Sergeant Lou Lowery, a *Leatherneck* magazine photographer, joined the patrol. After a short firefight, the 54" x 28" flag was attached to a piece of pipe found at the ridge of the mountain and was raised. This was the flag-raising that Staff Sergeant Lowery photographed. But this flag was too small to be seen from the beach below, and another Marine went on board *LST 779* to get a larger flag. Then, a second patrol took this flag up to the top of Suribachi, accompanied by AP photographer Joe Rosenthal.

In an interview after the war, Rosenthal said: "my stumbling on that picture was in all respects accidental. When I got to the top of the mountain, I stood in a decline just below the crest of the hill with Sergeant Bill Genaust, a motion picture cameraman (later killed on Iwo Jima). We watched a group of five Marines and a Navy corpsman fasten the new flag to another piece of pipe. I turned, and out of the corner of my eye, I saw the second flag being raised. I swung my camera around and held it until I could guess where the peak of the action was and then took the shot."

Some people accused Rosenthal's second flag-raising photograph of being posed. According to Rosenthal's postwar interview: "had I posed that shot, I would, of course, have ruined it. I would've made them turn their heads so they could be identified, and nothing like the existing picture would have resulted. This picture and what it meant to me—and it has a meaning to me—has to be peculiar only to me.

"I can still see blood running down the sand. I can see those awful, impossible positions to take in a frontal attack on such an island, where the batteries opposing you were not only staggered up in front of you but also stood around you as you came ashore. The extraordinary situation they were in before they ever reached that peak. If a photograph can remind us of the sacrifices these boys made—then that was what made the photo important—not the man who took it."

Rosenthal took eighteen photographs that day. Afterward, he went down to the beach to write captions for his undeveloped film packs and, with other photographers on the island, sent his film out to the offshore command vessel. They were flown to Guam, where the photos were processed and censored. Rosenthal's pictures arrived on Guam before Lowery's and were processed and sent to the states for distribution. Rosenthal's flag-raising picture became one of the most famous photographs ever taken in the war—or in any war.

ALLIED COMMANDERS

Four veteran Marine generals led the assault on Iwo Jima. Each one of these generals received the Distinguished Service Medal for inspired combat leadership in this epic battle.

* * *

Major General Harry Schmidt was fifty-eight years old when he was on Iwo Jima. He'd already served thirty-six years in the Marine Corps. Born and raised in Holdrege, Nebraska, he attended the Nebraska Normal College. His expeditionary assignments kept him from serving in World War I, but Schmidt saw considerable small unit action in China, the Philippines, Guam, Mexico, Nicaragua, and Cuba.

Schmidt attended the Army Command and General Staff College and the Marine Corps Field Officer's Course. During World War II, General Schmidt commanded the 4th Marine Division at Roi-Namur and in Saipan before assuming command of the V Amphibious Corps at the Tinian landing.

On Iwo Jima, he commanded the largest force of Marines ever committed to a single battle. According to Schmidt: "it was the greatest honor of my life."

* * *

Major General Graves B. Erskine was forty-seven years old on Iwo Jima, and one of the youngest major generals in the Marine Corps. He'd already served twenty-eight years on active duty by then. A native of Columbia, Louisiana, he received a Marine Corps commission after graduating from Louisiana State University.

Erskine immediately deployed to France for duty in World War I. He served as a platoon commander in the 6th Marines and saw combat at Chateau-Thierry, Soissons, St. Mihiel, and Belleau Wood. He was wounded twice and awarded the Silver Star. He served in China, Cuba, Nicaragua, Santo Domingo, and Haiti in the interwar period.

In World War II, Erskine was Chief of Staff to General Holland Smith during the Marianas, Marshalls, Gilberts, and Aleutians campaigns. He took command of the 3rd Marine Division in October 1944.

* * *

Major General Clifton B. Cates was fifty-one years old at Iwo Jima. He'd served the last twenty-eight years in the Marine Corps. Cates was one of the rare Marine general officers who had held a combat command at the platoon, company, battalion, regiment, and division levels in his career.

Cates was born in Tiptonville, Tennessee, and graduated from the University of Tennessee. In World War I, he served as a junior officer in the 6th Marines at Blanc Mont, Soissons, Belleau Wood, and St. Mihiel. He was awarded two Silver Stars, the Navy Cross, and a Purple Heart for his service and wounds.

In the interwar years, he served at sea and in China. In World War II, he commanded the 1st Marines at Guadalcanal and the 4th Marine Division at Tinian. Three years after Iwo Jima, General Clifton Cates became the 19th Commandant of the Marine Corps.

Major General Keller E. Rockey was fifty-six years old on Iwo Jima and a thirty-one-year veteran of the Marine Corps. A native of Columbia City, Indiana, he graduated from Gettysburg College and studied at Yale. Like his fellow division commanders, Rockey served in France in World War I and was awarded the Navy Cross as a junior officer in the 5th Marines at Chateau-Thierry.

He earned a second Navy Cross for heroic service in Nicaragua. He also served in Haiti and had two years of sea duty. After spending the first years of World War II at Marine Corps Headquarters in Washington, in February 1944, General Rockey took command of the 5th Marine Division and prepared them for their first and last great battle of the war.

* * *

Three other brigadier generals played a considerable role in the amphibious seizure of Iwo Jima:

- Leo Hermle, Assistant Division Commander of the 5th Marine Division.
- Franklin Hart, Assistant Division Commander of the 4th Marine Division.
- William Rogers, Corps Chief of Staff.

GENERAL KURIBAYASHI

According to Colonel Chambers, Battalion Commander of the 3/25 Marines, whose four days on Iwo Jima resulted in a Purple Heart and a Medal of Honor: "On Iwo, their smartest general commanded. This man did not believe in the banzai business. He ordered each Jap to kill ten Marines—and for a while, they made their quotas."

Chambers was referring to Lieutenant General Kuribayashi, Commander of the *Ogasawara Army Group* and Commanding General of the *109th Division.* Tadamichi Kuribayashi was fifty-three years old on Iwo. He was from the Nagano Prefecture and served the Emperor as a cavalry officer since graduating from the Military Academy in 1914. Kuribayashi spent several years as a junior officer posted to the Japanese embassies in Canada and the United States. During the war in Asia, Kuribayashi commanded a cavalry regiment in Manchuria and a brigade in northern China. Later he served as Chief of Staff for the *Twenty-third Army* during the capture of Hong Kong.

After returning from China, the Emperor chose Kuribayashi to command the *Imperial Guards Division* in Tokyo. When Saipan fell in June 1944, he was assigned to command the defense of Iwo Jima.

Kuribayashi was a realist. He believed the crude airstrips on Iwo were a liability for the Empire. They provided nuisance raids against the B-29s but would undoubtedly draw attention from Allied strategic planners. The Iwo Jima airfields in Allied hands would pose a terrible threat to Japan.

Kuribayashi knew he had only two options: blow up the entire island or defend it to the death. Blowing up the entire island would be impractical, so he adopted a radical defensive policy. His troops would not use the suicidal banzai nor linear water's edge tactics used in previous island battles. This caused a massive controversy at the highest levels—Imperial headquarters even asked the Nazis for advice on how to repel American invasions.

While Kuribayashi made some compromises with his forces on the island, he fired eighteen senior army officers, including his chief of staff. Those who remained would implement Kuribayashi's policy to the letter.

The general knew he was doomed without air and naval support. Still, he proved to be a tenacious and resourceful commander. His only tactical error was in authorizing sector commanders to engage the Allied task force covering the UDT operations on D -2. This gift revealed to the gunners the masked batteries which would have slaughtered more of the landing force assault waves on D-Day.

Controversial Japanese accounts reported Kuribayashi committed *Seppuku* (Japanese ritual suicide) in his cave near Kitano point on March 23, 1945—the thirty-third day of battle. General

Holland Smith said: "of all our adversaries in the Pacific, Kuribayashi was the most redoubtable. Let's hope the Japs don't have any more like him."

JAPANESE SPIGOT MORTAR

One of the deadliest weapons faced on Iwo Jima was the 320mm spigot mortar. These gigantic defensive weapons were placed and operated by the Imperial Japanese Army's *20th Independent Mortar Battalion*.

The mortar tube had a small muzzle cavity. It rested on a steel base plate supported by a wooden platform. Unlike typical mortars, this five-foot-long projectile was placed over the tube instead of dropping down the barrel. The mortar shell's diameter was thirteen inches, while the tube was only a little more than ten inches wide.

This weapon hurled a 675-pound shell over 1,500 yards. The range was adjusted by varying the powder charge, while deflection changes were accomplished by brute force: pushing and shoving the base platform. Although tubes only held out for six rounds, enough shells were lobbed onto Allied positions to make a lasting impression.

A rifleman in the 28th Marines referred to it as "The Screaming Jesus." Most Marines had a healthy respect for the mortar. General Robert Cushman, who commanded the 2/9 Marines on Iwo Jima (later becoming the 25th Commandant of the Marine Corps), recalled the inaccuracy and terror of the tumbling projectiles: "you could see it coming. But you never knew where the hell it was going to come down."

IWO'S AIR SUPPORT

For a few memorable moments before the D-Day landing, the Marines' vision of an integrated air-ground assault team became a reality. As assault troops neared the beach in their tracked amphibian vehicles, dozens of F4U Corsairs swept in and paved the way with rockets and machine-gun fire. According to one Marine: "it was magnificent."

Unfortunately, the Marine fighter squadrons on Iwo Jima that morning came from the fast attack carriers of Task Force 58, not the amphibious task force. Three days later, Task Force 58 left for good in pursuit of more strategic targets. Following that, Navy and Army Air Force pilots provided support for the landing force fighting ashore. Sustained close air support of amphibious forces by Marine air was (once again) postponed for some future combat proving ground.

Other Marine aviation units contributed to the capture of Iwo Jima. One of the first to see action was VMB 612 (Marine Bombing Squadron) out of Saipan. Flight crews on PBJ Mitchell medium bombers ran long-range nightly rocket attacks against enemy ships trying to resupply. These nightly raids, along with the Navy's submarine interdictions, slashed the amount of ammunition and fortifications (mostly barbed wire) delivered to the enemy before the invasion.

Pilots and aerial spotters from Marine observation squadrons flew in from escort carriers or were launched from the infamous *LST 776's* slingshot. These crews played a crucial role in spotting enemy artillery and mortar positions and reporting them.

Marine transport aircraft based in the Marianas delivered critical combat cargo to the island at the height of the battle. Marines relied on aerial delivery before the landing force could establish a fully functional beachhead. On D +1, marine transport squadrons airdropped critically needed machine gun parts, mortar shells, and blood plasma within the lines. On March 3, Colonel Malcolm Mackay landed the first Marine transport aircraft on the island—a Curtiss Commando R5C loaded with ammunition. The three other Marine squadrons followed and brought in much-needed supplies and evacuated the wounded.

On March 8, Marine Torpedo Bomber Squadron 224 flew in from Tinian and took responsibility for day and night anti-submarine patrols. Colonel Vernon Megee had the honor of commanding the first Landing Force Air Support Control Unit (a landmark in the evolution of amphibious combat).

Megee came ashore on D +5 with General Schmidt, but the offloading process was still in such shambles that it took five days to gather communication jeeps. This did not deter Megee. He "borrowed" gear and moved inland to coordinate the Air Liaison Parties. He persuaded Navy pilots to use bigger bombs and listened to the assault commanders' complaints.

McGee's work in training and employing Army P-51 Mustang pilots was masterful. Kuribayashi transmitted to Tokyo "lessons learned" in defending against the Allied amphibious assault during the battle. One of his messages said: "the enemy's air control is strong. At least thirty aircraft flew ceaselessly from early morning to night over this very small island."

SHERMAN ZIPPO TANKS

For many Marines on Iwo Jima, the Sherman M4A3—with the Mark I flamethrower—was the most effective weapon employed in the battle.

On Iwo, Marines had come a long way with the tactical use of fire. Fifteen months earlier on Tarawa, only a handful of backpack flamethrowers were available to fight hundreds of the island's fortifications. While the assault force relied on portable flamethrowers, most Marines saw the value in marrying this technology with armored vehicles for use against the island's toughest targets.

In the Marianas, Marines modified M3A1 light tanks with the Canadian Ronson flame system to a deadly effect. But the small vehicles were vulnerable to enemy fire. On Peleliu, the 1st Marine Division mounted the improvised Mark I system on a thin skin LVT. But again, the vehicle's susceptibility to enemy fire limited the effectiveness of the system. The obvious solution was to mount the flamethrower on a tank.

Early modifications to the Shermans were made by replacing the bow machine gun with the small E4-5 mechanized flamethrower. Replacing the bow machine gun was only a minor improvement. The short-range, limited fuel supply and awkward aiming process did not compensate for losing the machine gun. Each of the three tank battalions used the E4-5-equipped Shermans on Iwo Jima.

The best solution for effective flame projection and mechanized mobility came from the Army's Chemical Warfare technicians on Hawaii before the invasion. Colonel Bill Collins, CO 5th Tank Battalion, inspired this tinkerer group to modify the Mark I flamethrower to operate within the Shermans' turret. By replacing the 75mm main gun with a look-alike launch tube, this modified system could be trained and pointed like any standard turret gun using napalm-thickened fuel. These Zippo tanks streamed 250 yards of flame for eighty seconds—a significant tactical improvement.

But the modification team only had enough time to modify eight M4A3 tanks with the Mark I flame system. The 4th and 5th Tank Battalions were each issued four. The 3rd Tank Battalion on Guam didn't receive any M4A3 Shermans nor field modifications in time for the battle on Iwo Jima. Although several of their A2 tanks kept the E4-5 system mounted in the bow.

The eight Sherman Zippo tanks were ideal against Iwo's rugged caves and concrete fortifications. The enemy was terrified of this weapon. Suicide squads of human bullets would attack flame tanks directly only to be shot down by covering forces or charred by napalm. Enemy fire took a toll on the eight flame tanks—but maintenance crews worked around the clock to keep them in the fight.

Captain Frank Caldwell, Company Commander of the 26th Marines said: "it was a flame tank more than any other supporting arm that won this battle."

The tactical demand for flame tanks never diminished. The 5th Tank Battalion used 10,000 gallons of napalm-thickened fuel a day. When the 5th Marine Division had cornered the last Japanese defenders in "The Gorge," their final after-action report stated the flame tank was one of the weapons that caused the enemy to leave their caves and rock crevices and run for their lives.

BUCK ROGERS MEN

Provisional rocket detachments were attached to the subdivisions of the landing force on Iwo Jima. Marines had a love-hate relationship with the little rocket trucks and their brave crews. These trucks were a one-ton, four wheel drive truck modified to carry three box-shaped rocket launchers containing a dozen 4.5-inch rockets.

Crews fired a ripple of thirty-six rockets within seconds and provided a carpet of high explosives on the target. While effective and deadly, each launch drew heavy return fire from the Japanese—who dreaded the automatic artillery.

The Experimental Rocket Unit was formed in June 1943 and first deployed rail-launched barrage rockets during the fighting in the Solomons. There, heavily canopied jungles limited their efficiency. But once mounted on trucks and deployed in the Central Pacific, these rockets were deadly and effective, especially during the battle on Saipan.

Marines reinforced the trucks' tailgate to serve as a blast shield. They installed hydraulic jacks to raise and lower the launchers. Crude steel rods were welded to the bumper and dashboard to help the driver align the vehicle with the aiming stakes.

A hilly treeless Iwo proved an ideal battleground for the "Buck Rogers Men." The 1st Provisional Rocket Detachment supported the 4th and 5th Marine Divisions throughout the battle on Iwo Jima. The Buck Rogers Men fired over 30,000 rockets to support the landing force.

The Rocket Detachment landed on Red Beach on D-Day and lost one vehicle in the surf and several others to heavy enemy fire or loose sand. When the first vehicle reached its firing position intact, it launched a salvo of rockets against Japanese fortifications on the slopes of Suribachi. It detonated an enemy ammunition dump. The detachment supported the Marines advance to the summit, often launching single rockets to clear suspected enemy positions along the route.

As the fighting advanced north, the rocket launchers' short-range deep angle fire and saturation effect kept them in high demand. They were effective in defilade-to-defilade bombardments. But the distinct flashing telltale blast always caught the attention of the Japanese artillery spotters. The rocket trucks rarely remained in one place long enough to fire more than two salvos. A fast displacement was critical to their survival. Marines knew better than to stand around and wave goodbye—it was time to seek deep shelter from the counter-battery fire sure to follow.

LOGISTICAL SUPPORT

The logistical effort necessary to sustain the assault force on Iwo Jima was complex, enormous, and learned from previous lessons in Pacific amphibious operations. No other element of the emerging art of amphibious warfare had improved so greatly by the winter of 1945.

While Marines had the courage and firepower to tackle a fortress like Iwo Jima, they would have been crippled without the available amphibious logistical support. The procedures, organizations, and concepts took years to develop. But once in place, they enabled the large-scale conquests on Iwo Jima and Okinawa.

On Iwo Jima, the 8th Field Depot was commanded by Colonel Leland Swindler. This depot served as the nucleus of shore party operations. Swindler coordinated the activities of all shore party operations. The logistical support on Iwo was well-conceived and executed. Liaison teams from the 8th Field Depot accompanied the 4th and 5th Divisions ashore. On D +3, field depot units came ashore, took over the unloading, and continued without interruption.

Every imaginable method of delivering combat cargo ashore was used. This involved "hot cargo," carried in by the assault waves. Hot cargo was preloaded in on assault waves or floating dumps. This experimental use of one-shot preloaded amphibious trailers, Wilson drums, and a general loading and unloading would be known to future generations as the "assault follow-on echelon."

Aerial delivery was first by parachute and then via transports landing on the captured runways. The Marine/Navy team experimented with the use of armored bulldozers and sleds loaded with hinged matting delivered by assault waves to clear wheeled vehicles stuck in the soft, volcanic sand. Despite fearsome obstacles: heavy surf, dangerous undertows, foul weather, and formidable enemy fire—the system worked. The combat cargo flowed in and kept casualties and salvaged equipment flowing out.

The occasional shortages were often the result of the

Marines meeting a more robust defensive garrison than initially expected. Urgent calls for more demolitions, grenades, mortar illumination rounds, and blood plasma were common. Transport squadrons delivered many of these critical items directly from the Mariana Islands fleet bases.

The field medical support on Iwo was a model of detailed planning and flexible application. Marines received immediate medical attention from their corpsmen and surgeons. But the system from hospitals to grave registration was mind boggling to some of the older veterans. Moderately wounded Marines received full hospital treatment and rehabilitation—often returning directly to their units—this preserved some of the swiftly decreasing combat experience levels in the frontline outfits. The more seriously wounded were stabilized, evacuated, and treated in offshore hospital ships or taken by air to Guam.

Marines fired an extraordinary half-million artillery rounds to support the assault units. Many rounds were lost when the 5th Marine Division's ammo dump blew up. But the flow never stopped. The shore party used LVTs and amphibious trucks for a fast offloading of ammunition ships dangerously exposed to enemy gunners. Marines helped the shore party hustle munitions onshore and into the neediest hands.

Colonel James Hittle of the 3rd Division (the reserve landing force) shook his head at the "crazy quilt" logistics adopted because of Iwo's geography. Hittle "appropriated" a transport plane and made regular runs to Guam—returning with fresh beef, beer, and mail. Colonel Hittle sent his transport quartermaster out to sea in an LVT full of war souvenirs to trade for bread, eggs, and fresh fruit.

Hittle was amazed at the density of troops funneled onto the small island: "at one point, we had over 60,000 men occupying less than three and a half miles of broken terrain." He directed Marine engineers to dig a well near the beach for a freshwater distilling plant. Instead of a saltwater source, engineers discovered steaming mineral water heated by Suribachi's dormant volcano.

Hittle moved the distilling site, and this spot became a hot shower facility—one of the most popular places on the island.

* * *

Building a relationship with my readers is one of the best things about writing. I occasionally send out emails with details on new releases and special offers. If you'd like to join my free readers group and never miss a new release, go to danielwrinn.com to sign up for the list.

ALSO BY DANIEL WRINN

Operation Iceberg: 1945 Victory on Okinawa (Book 9 in the Series)

"*An unforgettable read about the Pacific War's bloodiest battle and the significance of Okinawa.*" –Reader

A gripping account of the final campaign of World War II—the victory on Okinawa.

The invasion of Okinawa was the largest amphibious assault in the Pacific Theater. Codenamed Operation Iceberg, it was also one of the bloodiest battles in the Pacific, lasting ninety-eight days.

After a long campaign of island hopping, the Allies

planned to use Kadena Air Base on Okinawa as a base for Operation Downfall, the planned invasion of the Japanese home islands. This battle was also known as "typhoon of steel" [English translation], because of the ferocity of the fighting, the intensity of kamikaze attacks and the sheer numbers of Allied ships and armored vehicles that assaulted the island.

This narrative recounts the invasion of Okinawa in vivid, gritty detail. Explore the fascinating feats of strategy, planning, and bravery, handing the Allies what would eventually become a victory over the Pacific Theater and an end to Imperialist Japanese expansion.

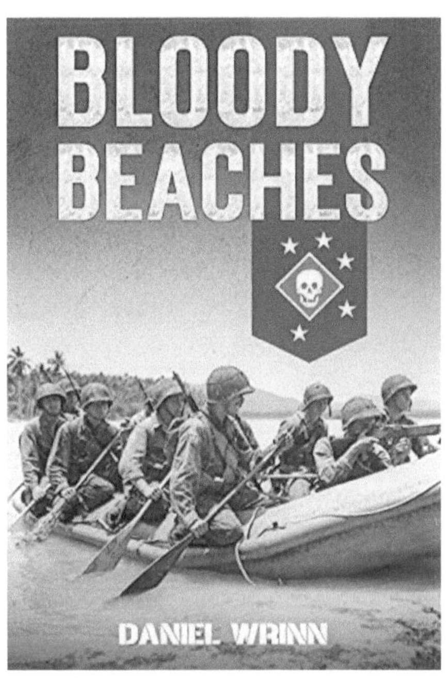

Bloody Beaches : Marine Raiders in World War II

"Great book for Marines, former Marines and history buffs!" – Reader

A powerful account of the Marine Raiders during World War II

Marine Raiders were special operations forces established during the Pacific campaign to conduct amphibious light infantry warfare. "Edson's" Raiders of 1st Marine Raider Battalion and "Carlson's" Raiders of 2nd Marine Raider Battalion were the first US special operations forces to form and see combat during World War II.

Despite the original intent for Raiders to serve in a special operations capacity, most combat operations saw the Raiders employed as conventional infantry. This, combined with the resentment within the rest of the Marine Corps that the Raiders were an "elite force within an elite force," led to the original Raider units being disbanded.

This narrative recounts the story of the Marine Raiders in vivid, gritty detail. Explore the fascinating feats of strategy, planning, and bravery, handing the Allies what would eventually become a victory over the Pacific Theater and an end to Imperialist Japanese expansion.

World War II Pacific: Battles and Campaigns from Guadalcanal to Okinawa 1942-1945

"A brisk and compelling game changer for the historiography of the Pacific Theater in World War II." – Reader

An enlightening glimpse into nine battles and campaigns during the Pacific War Allied offensive.

Each of these momentous operations were fascinating feats of strategy, planning, and bravery, handing the Allies what would eventually become a victory over the Pacific Theater and an end to Imperialist Japanese expansion.

Operation Watchtower, a riveting exploration of the spark that set off the Allied offensive in the Pacific islands, detailing the grueling struggle for the island of Guadalcanal and its vital strategic position.

Operation Galvanic, an incredible account of the battle for the Tarawa Atoll and base that would give them a steppingstone into the heart of Japanese-controlled waters.

Operation Backhander, a gripping retelling of the war for Cape Gloucester, New Guinea, and the Bismarck Sea.

Battle for Saipan, Marines stormed the beaches with a goal of gaining a crucial air base from which the US could launch its new long-range B-29 bombers directly at Japan's home islands.

Invasion of Tinian, is the incredible account of the assault on Tinian. Located just under six miles southwest of Saipan. This was the first use of napalm and the "shore to shore" concept.

Recapture of Guam, a gripping narrative about the liberation of the Japanese-held island of Guam, captured by the Japanese in 1941 during one of the first Pacific campaigns of the War.

Operation Stalemate, Marines landed on the island of Peleliu, one of the Palau Islands in the Pacific, as part of a larger operation to provide support for General MacArthur, who was preparing to invade the Philippines.

Operation Detachment, the battle of Iwo Jima was a major offensive in World War II. The Marine invasion was tasked with the mission of capturing airfields on the island for use by P-51 fighters.

Operation Iceberg, the invasion and ultimate victory on Okinawa was the largest amphibious assault in the Pacific Theater. It was also one of the bloodiest battles in the Pacific, lasting ninety-eight days.

This gripping narrative sheds light on these often-overlooked facets of WWII, providing students, history fans, and World War II buffs alike with a captivating breakdown of the history and combat that defined the ultimate victory of US forces in the Pacific.

REFERENCES

Alexander, Colonel Joseph. "'In for One Hell of a Time': Bloody Sacrifice at the Battle of Iwo Jima." HistoryNet.com and World War II magazine. HistoryNet.com and World War II magazine, February 2000.

Allen, Robert E. *The First Battalion of the 28th Marines on Iwo Jima: a Day-by-Day History from Personal Accounts and Official Reports, with Complete Muster Rolls*. McFarland, 1999.

"Amphibious Operations: Capture of Iwo Jima." Naval History and Heritage Command, October 23, 2019.

Antill, Peter D. "The Battle for Iwo Jima." History of War, April 6, 2001.

Bradley, James, and Ron Powers. *Flags of Our Fathers*. New York: Bantam Books, 2006.

Bradley, James. *Flyboys: a True Story of American Courage*. Boston: Little, Brown, 2003.

Buell, Hal. *Uncommon Valor, Common Virtue: Iwo Jima and the Photograph That Captured America*. New York, NY: Berkley, 406AD.

Burrell, Robert S. *The Ghosts of Iwo Jima*. College Station: Texas A&M University Press, 2006.

Hammel, Eric M. *Iwo Jima: Portrait of a Battle: United States Marines at War in the Pacific*. St. Paul, MN: Zenith Press, 2006.

Hearn, Chester G. *Sorties into Hell: The Hidden War on Chichi Jima*. Guilford, CT: Lyons Press, 2005.

HistoricalResources. "Ivo Jima Maps - February 19, 1945–March 26, 1945." Historical Resources About The Second World War RSS, September 15, 2008.

Horie, Yoshitaka, Robert D. Eldridge, and Charles W. Tatum. *Fighting Spirit: The Memoirs of Major Yoshitaka Horie and the Battle of Iwo Jima*. Annapolis, MD: Naval Institute Press, 2011.

Kindersley, Dorling. *World War II: The Definitive Visual History*. New York: DK Publishing, 2009.

Salomon, Henry. *Victory at Sea Volume 23: Target Suribachi*. United States of America: The National Broadcasting Company, 1954.

Shively, John C. *The Last Lieutenant: A Foxhole View of the Epic Battle for Iwo Jima*. Bloomington: Indiana University Press, 2006.

Sperling, Milton. *To the Shores of Iwo Jima*. United States of America: United States Navy and United States Marine Corps, 1945.

Toll, Ian W. *TWILIGHT OF THE GODS: War in the Western Pacific, 1944-1945*. S.l.: W W NORTON, 2020.

Veronee, Marvin D. *A Portfolio of Photographs: Selected to Illustrate the Setting for My Experience in the Battle of Iwo Jima, World War II, Pacific Theater, as a Naval Gunfire Liaison Officer with the First Battalion, 28th Marines, 19 February-26 March 1945*. Quantico: Visionary Pub., 2001.

Wells, Keith. *Give Me Fifty Marines Not Afraid to Die: Iwo Jima*. Abilene, TX: Produced by Quality Publications, 1995.

Wheeler, Richard. *Iwo*. Annapolis, MD: Naval Institute Press, 1994.

World War 2 Pictures. "Iwo Jima Pictures." WW2-Pictures.-com, April 16, 2010.

Wright, Derrick. *Iwo Jima 1945: The Marines Raise the Flag On Mount Suribachi*. Oxford: Osprey Publishing Ltd, 2004.

"Breaking the Cycle of Iwo Jima Mythology: A Strategic Study of Operation Detachment." *The Journal of Military History* 68, no. 4 (October 2004)

The Battle for Iwo Jima 1945. Stroud: Sutton, 2006.

"'Rare Photos of the Battle of Iwo Jima from the U.S. National Archives and the Department of Defense, USMC.'" Awesome Stories. Accessed June 2021.

ABOUT THE AUTHOR

Daniel Wrinn writes Military History & War Stories. A US Navy veteran and avid history buff, Daniel lives in the Utah Wasatch Mountains. He writes every day with a view of the snow capped peaks of Park City to keep him company. You can join his readers group and get notified of new releases, special offers, and free books here:

www.danielwrinn.com

www.ingramcontent.com/pod-product-compliance
Ingram Content Group UK Ltd.
Pitfield, Milton Keynes, MK11 3LW, UK
UKHW041853190726
13854UKWH00002B/869